A survey of the current situation in ASEAN

VOLUNTARY AND COMPULSORY ARBITRATION OF LABOUR DISPUTES

Published under the auspices of the
joint ILO/UNDP/ASEAN Programme of Industrial
Relations for Development

ISBN 92-2-106377-1
First published 1988

CONTENTS

FOREWORD

One of the important objectives of the ASEAN Programme on Industrial Relations for Development (RAS/81/033) – a joint project of UNDP, ASEAN, and the ILO – was to promote the study and analysis of basic issues in labour relations and labour laws within the ASEAN countries. To meet this objective a number of national experts have been invited under the Project to prepare country studies on the following issues:

– The Problem of Union Recognition

– The Administration and Enforcement of Collective Agreements

– The Voluntary and Compulsory Arbitration of Labour Disputes

– The Right to Strike and Lockout

These studies have now been completed and are being published to provide an opportunity for students, practitioners, policy-makers to acquire valuable insights based on the experience of the ASEAN countries. It is hoped that these materials being published will promote comparative studies in labour relations and labour laws which in turn could lead to cross-fertilisation of ideas and concepts and even to desirable reforms.

We deeply regret that the materials from Indonesia could not be included in this publication due to time constraints.

On behalf of the ILO, let me express our appreciation to the various authors who have taken the time and effort in this worthwhile endeavour.

This series of publications on basic issues in labour relations and labour laws in the ASEAN countries has been made possible due to the support of the United Nations Development Programme (UNDP) and ASEAN under the ASEAN Programme of Industrial Relations for Development Project. The ILO feels privileged to have served as the Executing Agency of the Project.

S. Nakatani
Assistant Director-General
responsible for ILO activities
in Asia and the Pacific

Bangkok, Thailand
March 1988

VOLUNTARY AND COMPULSORY ARBITRATION OF LABOUR DISPUTES IN NEGARA BRUNEI DARUSSALAM

by
Mr. R. Thiagarajah, ILO Consultant

INTRODUCTION

There is a continuing search in many Asian countries for the most suitable machinery and procedures that will provide speedy settlement of various kinds of labour disputes. Traditional settlement procedures, however, are still the most common. These consist of three consecutive steps:

- bipartite discussions,
- conciliation or mediation, and
- arbitration; usually divided into voluntary and compulsory arbitration.

While these procedures were originally applied to all types of disputes, a growing number of countries have recently attempted to set up special procedures for the settlement of so called "rights disputes". These arise between individual workers and their employers out of alleged unfair dismissals or other grievances. While reserving the right of the parties to opt for voluntary arbitration, the government is empowered to refer any labour dispute to arbitration on its own motion under certain circumstances.

Compulsory arbitration in most of these countries is entrusted to courts. These are known by various names, such as labour courts, industrial tribunals, industrial courts or industrial arbitration courts. They are made up mostly of persons who have been, or who are qualified to be, judges in ordinary courts. Arbitration courts in a number of countries are constituted on a tripartite basis providing for equal representation of employers' and workers' interests. Although voluntary arbitration is not a preferred means of disputes settlement in Asian countries, collective agreements concluded in some of them provide it as the final step in the settlement of disputes arising from the application and interpretation of the agreements.

LEGAL POSITION

TRADE DISPUTES ENACTMENT

In Negara Brunei Darussalam, the settlement of labour disputes is governed by the provisions of the Trade Disputes Enactment No. 6 of 1961 (hereinafter referred to as the "Enactment"). This provides for a voluntary system of disputes settlement based on the British tradition. The disputes settlement machinery and procedures established by the Enactment are made applicable not only to workers in the private sector, but also to government workers other than the armed forces, the police force and the prison service.

Trade Dispute

Under the Enactment, a "trade dispute" is defined as: –

> "any dispute between employers and workers, or between workers and workers connected with the employment, non-employment, or the terms of the employment or with the conditions of work of any person".

The scope of the definition is so wide that it encompasses both "rights" and "interests" disputes. The matter of a dispute can relate to a person's employment, his suspension or interdiction from work, disciplinary issues, dismissals, application or interpretation of the existing terms of employment, improvement of such terms of employment, union recognition and related issues, matters concerning working conditions, superannuation benefits and so forth. The parties to a dispute need not always be workers and employers. A dispute can also arise between workers and workers. Disputes concerning claims for recognition by two or more competing unions can be a typical example of such a dispute.

Procedures and Machinery

Three consecutive steps are provided in the Enactment for the settlement of labour disputes: namely, bipartite discussions, conciliation and voluntary arbitration. The freedom of the parties to establish their own arrangements for dispute settlement is made explicit in section 16 of the Enactment:

"16. If there are existing in any trade or industry arrangements for settlement by conciliation or arbitration of disputes in such trade or industry, or any branch thereof, made in pursuance of an agreement between organisations of employers and organisations of workers representative respectively of substantial proportions of the employers and workers engaged in that trade or industry –

(a) the Mentri Besar* shall not, unless and until there has been a failure to obtain settlement by means of these arrangements, refer the matter in dispute in accordance with the provisions of section 19; and

---

* Mentri Besar means Chief Minister

(b) the Commissioner of Labour shall not, unless and until there has been a failure to obtain settlement by means of these arrangements, exercise his powers under paragraph (4) of sub-section (1) of section 17."

What do the provisions of section 16 imply? Firstly, the parties have the right to establish their own procedures and machinery for the settlement of disputes arising between them. Secondly, it is possible for the parties to establish their own machinery for conciliation and arbitration independent of the State machinery. Thirdly, the state arbitration machinery can be invoked only on the failure of the parties to obtain a settlement in accordance with the conciliation and arbiration procedures established by them under an existing agreement.

But it has to be noted that the provisions of section 16 will not apply to all disputes. For these provisions to be applied, there must be in existence between the parties to a dispute an agreement providing for the settlement of disputes by conciliation or arbitration; and such parties shall be an organisation of workers and an organisation of employers sufficiently representative respectively of the whole or substantial proportions of the workers and employers engaged in the industry or trade concerned. Such an arrangement would not be possible in the State due to the absence of any employers' organisation. Hence, in the present state of affairs the Commissioner of Labour and the Mentri Besar are free to invoke the provisions of sections 17 and 18 of the Enactment, respectively, for purposes of settling any trade dispute.

Role of the Commissioner

Where the parties fail to obtain settlement of a dispute in accordance with the agreed procedure, section 17 (1) of the Enactment requires the Commissioner of Labour to intervene with the object of promoting settlement by conciliation:

"17 (1). Where a trade dispute exists or is apprehended the Commissioner of Labour, with the object of promoting settlement by conciliation, shall –

(a) enquire into the causes and circumstances of the dispute;

(b) take such steps as to him may seem expedient for the purpose of enabling the parties to the dispute to meet together by themselves, or their representatives, with a view to amicable settlement of the dispute; and

(c) subject to the provisions of section 16, to appoint a person to act as conciliator, such person being, if possible, a person mutually agreed upon by both the employers and workers interested".

Under these provisions, the Commissioner of Labour can either promote a settlement of the dispute by himself or appoint a conciliator to bring about a settlement. Such an appointment can, however, be made only where the parties have already exhausted their own conciliation and arbitration machinery, where such arrangement exists. The Commissioner's right of intervention extends to both "existing" and "apprehended" disputes. In the absence of any specific provisions in the Enactment, it is possible for the Commissioner to intervene in any dispute, including an apprehended dispute, on his own motion or at the instance of the parties concerned or on the directive of the Mentri Besar.

The right of intervention in "apprehended" disputes will enable the Commissioner to intervene in a dispute at any stage, even during the stage of direct negotiations between the parties, with a view to preventing a dispute. This objective is reflected in para. (b) of sub-section (1) of section 17 which requires the Commissioner to take steps which will enable the parties to "meet together by themselves or their representatives, with a view to amicable settlement". In this respect, the function of the Commissioner, approximates to "preventive conciliation".

Formal Conciliation

The Commissioner is also authorised to appoint a conciliator to bring about a settlement of a trade dispute. Where possible, the Commissioner is required to appoint as conciliator, a "person mutually agreed upon by both the employers and workers interested". This provision will enable the Commissioner to appoint a conciliator who will command the confidence and support of both labour and management, an essential attribute of an effective conciliator. The appointment of a conciliator by mutual consent of the parties will, no doubt, enhance the success of the conciliator in settlement of any dispute.

A conciliator appointed by the Commissioner of Labour is required to inquire into the causes and circumstances of the trade dispute and "by negotiation with the parties endeavour to bring about a settlement". Where a settlement is reached, the parties are required to sign a memorandum of settlement embodying the terms of settlement. A copy of the Memorandum of Settlement shall be forwarded to the Commissioner of Labour by the conciliator.

A Memorandum of Settlement is not legally binding on the parties and is therefore not enforceable at law. It can only be considered as a "gentlemen's agreement", and the parties are expected to honour its terms in the same spirit in which it was concluded and signed by them.

The Mentri Besar is also given certain powers under the Enactment to promote a settlement of existing and apprehended trade disputes. Where such disputes are brought to his notice by the parties, the Mentri Besar is required by section 18 of the Enactment to "take the matter into consideration and take such steps as seem to him expedient for promoting a settlement thereof".

Arbitration Tribunal

One of the possible steps which the Mentri Besar could take is to refer the dispute, with the consent of both parties, to an arbitration tribunal. As in the case of appointment of a conciliator, reference to an arbitration tribunal can be made only after the parties have failed to obtain a settlement of the dispute by means of conciliation or arbitration under an existing agreed disputes settlement procedure.

An arbitration tribunal may be constituted of either –

- a sole arbitrator appointed by the Sultan;
- an arbitrator appointed by the Sultan, assisted by one or more assessors nominated by or on behalf of the employers concerned and an equal number of assessors nominated by or on behalf of the workers concerned, all of whom shall be appointed by the Sultan; or
- one or more arbitrators nominated by or on behalf of the employers concerned and an equal number of arbitrators nominated by or on behalf of the workers concerned, and an independent Chairman, all of whom shall be appointed by the Sultan (Section 19).

Where all members of the tribunal are unable to agree as to the award, the Chairman is empowered to take a decision as sole arbitrator. The rules of procedure to be followed by the tribunal may be regulated by the Sultan and where any matter has not been regulated, the tribunal shall regulate its own procedure.

The tribunal is vested with the same power as the High Court to require any person to furnish in writing or otherwise, such information relating to the dispute as the tribunal may require, to require the production of documents and, where necessary, to attend before the tribunal and give evidence on oath or otherwise, so as to elicit necessary facts and information relevant to the dispute, without being bound by the rules of evidence in civil or criminal proceedings.

The appearance of lawyers in any proceedings before the tribunal is permitted at the discretion of the tribunal. Likewise, the tribunal may allow the public or press to be present at a sitting at its discretion.

Where the press is allowed to be present in a sitting of a tribunal, a fair and accurate report or summary of the proceedings, including the evidence adduced at the sitting, may be published, after the publication of the award by order of the Mentri Besar. Any information as to any trade union or individual business obtained by the tribunal at a sitting where the press or public has been excluded shall not be included in the award or otherwise disclosed, except with the consent of the secretary of the trade union or the person, firm or company, as the case may be.

An award of the tribunal shall be submitted to the Mentri Besar who shall cause the same to be published in such manner as he thinks fit. If any question as to the interpretation of the award arises, any party to the award or the Mentri Besar may apply to the tribunal for a decision on such question, and the tribunal shall decide the matter after hearing the parties or without such hearing, provided the consent of the parties has been first obtained. The decision of the tribunal shall be notified to the parties and shall be deemed to form part of and shall have the same effect in all respects as the original award.

The award of the arbitration tribunal is not made legally binding on the parties and hence it is not possible to enforce it in a court of law. Its observance by the parties is therefore voluntary.

FACTUAL POSITION

Over three-fourths of the workers in Brunei Darussalam are employed in small establishments having less than 10 workers.[1] The employer-worker relationship in these establishments is very much on a personal basis. The workers generally enjoy favourable working conditions[2]. Brunei Petroleum Shell Co. Ltd. (BSP) is the second largest employer, next to the Government, employing about 4,000 workers.

Brunei Oilfields Workers' Union (BOWU) has successfully concluded collective agreements with the BSP once in three years since 1969.[3] These agreements, inter alia, provide for the settlement of disputes arising from the application of the agreement. The grievance procedure under the agreement envisages three steps for the disposal of collective grievances, and five steps for individual grievances. Once the procedure is exhausted, the parties to collective grievances can have recourse to the disputes settlement machinery established under the Trade Disputes Enactment.[4] The Grievance Procedures embodied in the BOWU-BSP collective agreement are reproduced in Annex A.

Although three other trade unions exist in the public sector, their membership is very low and their activities are confined to cultural and social matters. Moreover, they are, "qualified, so to speak, for deregistration".[5]

---

[1] Labour Protection and Labour Relations in ASEAN, Page 38.

[2] Prevention and Settlement of Labour Disputes in ASEAN, Page 60.

[3] Labour Relations in Public Enterprises in ASEAN, Page 6.

[4] Ibid.

[5] Collective Bargaining in Brunei Darussalam; a Country Paper presented at the 3rd Programme Advisory Committee Meeting of ASEAN/UNDP/ILO Programme on Industrial Relations for Development, 22-24 May, 1985.

Not a single collective dispute has ever been raised by any party with the Department of Labour.[6] All the trade disputes reported to the Department were "rights disputes" involving dismissals, statutory claims or contractual rights of individual workers:[7]

Trade Disputes 1980-1984

	1980	*1981*	*1982*	*1983*	*1984*
1. Dismissal without notice	7	55	45	89	32
2. Failure to pay wages	–	14	10	25	1
3. Failure to pay overtime	–	4	–	5	3
4. Deduction of wages	–	5	–	3	1
5. Other wage disputes	7	7	13	10	4
6. Miscellaneous disputes	9	14	22	29	5

About 60 per cent of these claims were settled through conciliation by Department officials, while the remaining cases were either settled amicably between the parties themselves or rejected by the Department on justifiable grounds.[8] Thus, the need has never arisen for the appointment of a conciliator by the Commissioner of Labour or an arbitration tribunal by the Mentri Besar under the provisions of the Trade Disputes Enactment.

CONCLUSIONS

To summarise –

– The disputes settlement procedures and machinery are established under the Trade Disputes Enactment No. 6 of 1961;

– The Enactment provides for three steps in the disputes settlement procedure; namely, bipartite discussions, conciliation and voluntary arbitration;

– The function of conciliation may be discharged by the Commissioner of Labour himself or by a conciliator appointed by him, if possible with the mutual consent of the parties;

– The function of voluntary arbitration is assigned to an arbitration tribunal appointed by the Mentri Besar;

---

6 Brunei Darussalam Country Paper for ASEAN Meeting on Labour Relations and Productivity at the Enterprise Level, Singapore 2-5, December 1986.

7 Labour Protection and Labour Relations in ASEAN, Pages 44-46.

8 Ibid. 39

- The settlement reached in conciliation proceedings and the award made by an arbitration tribunal are not made legally binding on the parties concerned and are, therefore, not enforceable at law;

- All trade disputes reported to the Department of Labour are rights disputes concerning claims of individual workers;

- About 60 per cent of these claims have been settled by conciliation, while the remaining cases have been either settled amicably between the parties or rejected by the Department as unfounded;

- The need has never arisen to invoke the provisions of the Enactment for the appointment of a conciliator or an arbitration tribunal;

- A compulsory arbitration system does not exist in the State.

GRIEVANCE PROCEDURES AT BSP

It is the intention of both the Company and the Union that grievances should be resolved as speedily and as effectively as possible. Specific grievances or complaints should be raised as soon as possible, and normally not later than 7 days after the event that gives rise to them.

Individual Grievances

Stage 1

An employee who has a grievance or claim will make this known in the first instance to his immediate Supervisor. The Supervisor will attempt to resolve the issue not later than three (3) full working days from the time when it was raised with him by the employee.

Stage 2

If the grievance is not resolved at Stage 1 the employee may take the matter up with his Division/Section Head who will attempt to resolve the matter not later than a further four (4) full working days from the time that the issue was raised with the Division/Section Head.

Stage 3

If the grievance is still unresolved at Stage 2 the employee may raise it with the Department Head concerned. The Department Head will attempt to resolve the matter not later than four (4) full working days from the time that the issue was raised with the Department Head. The employee may be accompanied by a Union Representative if he so wishes.

Stage 4

In the event that the foregoing process fails, the employee himself may present his case in writing to the Company's Representative for Union Affairs, who will endeavour to resolve the matter not later than six (6) full working days from the time that the issue was raised with him.

At this stage the employee may be accompanied by a Union Representative.

Where evidence is required from an employee who works offshore, up to seven (7) further days may be taken at each of the above stages.

Stage 5

In the event that the foregoing process fails, the employee himself may present his case in writing to the Company's Managing Director or his delegate whose decision will be final provided that such decision is not considered by the Complainant to be contrary to his Agreement. At this stage the employee may be assisted by a Union Representative.

Collective Grievances

Stage 1

A group of employees having a grievance may take the matter up at the supervisory level immediately below the Department Head concerned. They may be accompanied by a Union Representative if they so wish.

Stage 2

If the grievance is not resolved at Stage 1, the employees may raise it with the Department Head concerned. A Union Representative may accompany the group if they so wish.

Stage 3

If the grievance is unresolved in Stage 2, the employees or the Union may take the matter up with the Company Representative for Union Affairs. The employees may be accompanied by a Union Representative if they so wish.

Where evidence is required from an employee who works offshore, up to seven (7) further days may be taken at each of the above stages.

Conciliation

In the event that either of the foregoing processes fails to resolve the grievance(s), both the Company and the Union will have the right to refer the dispute to the Commissioner of Labour for conciliation.

Arbitration

If the dispute still remains unresolved after conciliation proceedings by the Commissioner of Labour, both parties agree to refer the dispute for settlement under the provisions of the Trade Dispute Enactment.

VOLUNTARY AND COMPULSORY ARBITRATION OF LABOUR DISPUTES IN MALAYSIA

by

Tengku Omar bin Tengku Bot,
Director of Industrial Relations,
Ministry of Labour, Malaysia.

INTRODUCTION

Disputes are a characteristic of human society. They fall into various categories and occur at different levels of relationship. Industrial relations are as dispute-prone as any other type of human relationship. Most systems of industrial relations in which employers and workers together seek to regulate their dealings with each other, and particularly to determine terms and conditions of employment, presuppose the possibility of disagreement and dispute. Disputes between employers and workers concerning their respective rights and interests are as old and common as employment itself. As industrialisation progressed, it became evident that labour disputes could be detrimental both to the stability of national economies and to the parties themselves. As a result, procedures were needed to assist the parties to settle their disputes. The importance of an appropriate settlement system adapted to the needs of each country is widely accepted today.

The two main methods of dispute settlement involving intervention of a third party are first, conciliation and mediation and second, arbitration. Conciliation, mediation and arbitration were used in dispute settlement between nations before the world became acquainted with the type of labour disputes generated by the Industrial Revolution. However, since the last decade of the nineteenth century, it is in industrial relations that these methods have been most widely, frequently and intensively applied.

In Malaysia, the existing industrial relations system operates within the legal framework of the Industrial Relations Act, 1967 which contains provisions for a three-stage settlement procedure; the stages are negotiation, conciliation and arbitration. The orderly stage by stage process starting from direct negotiation to conciliation and finally to arbitration forms the basis of dispute settlement procedure in Malaysia. The Industrial Relations Act, 1967 promotes and facilitates negotiations by providing adequate ground rules for collective bargaining. Where direct negotiation between the disputing parties does not result in agreement, conciliation has come to be accepted as a logical continuation of the negotiation process. The conciliation service provided by the Department of Industrial Relations under the Ministry of Labour functions effectively as is clearly reflected by its ability to settle over 80 per cent of trade disputes reported to it each year. With the main bulk of trade disputes settled at the conciliation stage, only about 12 per cent of total trade disputes need to go to the final stage of arbitration.

DEVELOPMENT OF INDUSTRIAL ARBITRATION LAWS

Industrial arbitration courts or tribunals were first established in this country in 1940 when the Industrial Courts Ordinance 1940 set up an Industrial Court in the Straits Settlements and the Industrial Courts Enactment 1940 set up another Industrial Court in the Federated Malay States. In 1941 an Industrial Court was also established in Kedah, one of the Non-Federated Malay States, by a State Enactment of 1940. However, the onset of World War II aborted the operation and development of these industrial tribunals.

After the war had ended and the Federation of Malaya formed, an Industrial Court was established by the Industrial Courts Ordinance 1948. The Ordinance also abolished the earlier tribunals in the Straits Settlements, the Federated Malay States and the State of Kedah by repealing the relevant legislation. The 1948 Industrial Court consisted of three panels made up respectively from independent persons, persons representing employers and worker representatives. The Court was headed by a President who had to be selected from the panel of independent persons. The President determined which members from the employers' and workers' panels (one from each panel) were to constitute the court in order to deal with any matter referred to it. Reference to the Court could be made only with the joint consent of the parties to the dispute. The Court's awards were not legally binding they were only "morally" so. The 1948 Industrial Court existed till the Industrial Relations Act, 1967 abolished it. In its 20-year span of existence it made only 18 awards.

Subsequently, the Industrial Arbitration Tribunal was established by the Essential (Arbitration in Essential Services) Regulations in March 1965 made under the Emergency (Essential Powers) Act 1964. The Tribunal was reconstituted by the Essential (Trade Disputes in the Essential Services) Regulations in September 1965 made under the same Act. (The September 65 Regulations repealed and replaced the March '65 Regulations). From the time it was established, the 1965 Industrial Tribunal virtually monopolised the industrial arbitration scene. It enjoyed jurisdiction over all labour-management disputes in the broadly defined "Essential Services". The Minister for Labour was empowered to use his sole discretion to refer a dispute to the Tribunal for arbitration if such dispute could not be resolved voluntarily either through negotiation or conciliation. Nearly every dispute was referred to the 1965 Industrial Tribunal, whose awards were binding on the parties, rather than to the still-existing 1948

Industrial Court which could only make non-binding awards. The 1965 Industrial Tribunal flourished till the Industrial Relations Act, 1967 abolished it. In its span of existence of only two years it made 35 awards.

Finally, the Industrial Relations Act, 1967 came into force on 7th August, 1967. This important Act, besides abolishing the 1948 Industrial Court and the 1965 Industrial Tribunal (by repealing the relevant legislation and regulations) also created the present arbitration tribunal, the 1967 Industrial Court.

Thus, there have only been three industrial arbitration courts or tribunals in Malaysia, namely, the 1948 Industrial Court, the 1965 Industrial Arbitration Tribunal, and the 1967 Industrial Court which continues to operate until today. Currently, besides the 1967 Industrial Court, the Labour Court established under the Employment Act 1965 also has jurisdiction over labour-management disputes. However, the Labour Court is not an arbitration tribunal. It is a special court constituted to inquire into and to decide certain complaints originating mainly from unorganised workers. The Court determines, more or less judicially, whether or not these complaints disclose a failure on the part of the employers to provide specified statutory or contractual benefits to their workers. If an infringement is found, the Court remedies it by ordering appropriate payment of such benefits. Although the Labour Court is not a court of law, its procedures correspond to those followed in the civil courts. It is guided by the Subordinate Court Rules. Labour Court decisions are enforceable in civil court. Either party which is not satisfied with a Labour Court decision has the right of appeal to the High Court.

TRANSITION FROM VOLUNTARY TO COMPULSORY ARBITRATION

It is clear therefore that the development and changes in industrial legislation have played key roles in shaping industrial relations in Malaysia. Within a comparatively short period of just over four decades, industrial arbitration in Malaysia has been completely transformed by stages from a voluntary to a compulsory system. The transformation was required chiefly due to changes in the political, social and economic patterns that had taken place during the period.

Historically, three distinct periods are discernible in the transition of Malaysia's industrial relations from a voluntary to a compulsory system. The first period was from 1946 to 1965, the second period from 1965 to 1967, and the third period from 1967 to the present day.

The first period, which began with the end of World War II and the emergence of trade unions, spanned a period of nineteen years during which the country also became an independent nation on 31st August 1957. This was the period of the voluntary system which was developed as an ad-hoc model from the British pattern in the late 1940's. The role of government during this period was mainly to supplement, when necessary, the voluntary arrangements which both sides in industry had made for themselves. The only legislation regulating the conduct of industrial relations during this period was the Industrial Court Ordinance 1948, the Trade Disputes Ordinance 1949, and the Trade Union Enactment 1940 which was subsequently replaced by the Trade Union Ordinance 1949. The Industrial Court Ordinance 1948 provided for the setting up of a standing industrial court from which disputing parties could voluntarily request arbitration of their disputes with non-binding awards. The Trade Disputes Ordinance 1949 required, inter alia, the giving of fourteen days' notice before a strike or a lockout could be called in an "essential service". The Trade Union Ordinance 1949 (and its predecessor – the Trade Union Enactment 1940) provided the legal framework for the formation and functioning of trade unions. The concept of voluntarism and autonomy which formed the main characteristic feature of the system was reflected not only in arbitration but also in collective bargaining; where acceptance of and adherence to collective agreements were only moral obligations. Thus, at that time, the whole machinery of labour dispute settlement was on a voluntary basis.

During the later part of the first period, the country having attained political independence in 1957 and the Emergency Administration of 1948-1960 having ended, trade unionism expanded. It also became more militant in a more permissive political climate. Industrial relations thus took a new turn towards instability and disharmony. Both sides in industry were beginning to ignore the normally accepted methods of maintaining cordial employer-employee relations, either by tending to stick uncompromisingly to their rights and prerogatives, or inclining to rely on the use of their position and strength to achieve their own aims and objectives. The situation deteriorated during 1964 and 1965. The nation, meanwhile, had been put on a state of emergency due to an external threat to its security from a neighbouring country. The result was a sharp increase in trade disputes and strikes which began to have an unfavourable effect on the national economy. To counteract this the government promulgated, in May 1965, the Essential (Prohibition of Strikes and Proscribed Industrial Actions) Regulations and the Essential (Arbitration in Essential Services) Regulations under the emergency powers of the Emergency (Essential Powers) Act 1964. These regulations, the promulgation of which marked the beginning of the second period, prohibited government employees from all forms of industrial action. The Minister of Labour was empowered to proscribe any industrial action in the private and quasi-public sector if the tendency of such action was to cause annoyance or inconvenience to the public. The Minister was also empowered to exercise his sole discretion to refer any trade dispute in any of the prescribed essential services (almost all services relating to health, economy and security of the country were classified as essential services) to the Industrial Arbitration Tribunal established under these Regulations for settlement, if the parties were unable to settle such dispute amicably through negotiation or conciliation. Any form of industrial action was proscribed once a trade dispute had been referred to the Tribunal for arbitration. In September of the same year, the two Regulations were superceded by the Essential (Trade Dispute in Essential Services) Regulations which contained additional provisions strengthening the basic concept of compulsory arbitration. For the first time in the history of the country, compulsory arbitration was introduced to settle trade disputes.

The 1965 Emergency Regulations were originally intended to be used as a temporary measure only. However, when the emergency ended in August 1966, new policies connected with the need for accelerated economic development through private investment emerged. A major study was carried out by the government to implement the policies. This study, which included a comprehensive review of existing laws and practices relating to industrial relations, pointed out that reliance on the goodwill of the parties alone would not be adequate to ensure industrial harmony. There was a need, in order to attract foreign and local private investment, for more active participation from the government so that it could play the peacemaker more effectively. This new thinking resulted in the Industrial Relations Act 1967, ushering in the third and final period of transition in Malaysia's industrial relations system. With the promulgation of the Act, compulsory arbitration became permanently entrenched in the Malaysian system of industrial relations.

CONSTITUTION OF THE INDUSTRIAL COURT

The Industrial Court consists of a President appointed by the Yang di Pertuan Agong (the King) and a panel of members. There are three categories of panel members, viz, independent persons, employers' representatives and workmen's representatives. All members of the panel are appointed by the Minister of Labour who may, before appointing them, consult such organisations representing employers and workmen as he may think fit. The Minister is also empowered to revoke at any time the appointment of any person to such panel without assigning any reason for doing so.

When the Court is dealing with any trade dispute, it is constituted of the President and three members selected by the Minister of Labour: one from each of the three categories. If any member, other than the President, is unable to attend or continue to attend any proceedings of the Court, the Minister may select another member from the appropriate category to fill the vacancy. The same procedure applies when a person ceases to be a member midway through a proceeding. However, the Court may act notwithstanding any vacancy in its number or in the absence of any member, other than the President, provided the parties to the dispute consent.

The Court may sit in two or more Divisions with the same or different Chairman appointed by the Yang di Pertuan Agong. The constitution of any Division is the same as when the Court sits under a President.

A President or Chairman of the Court may sit alone without any of the panel members when dealing with a matter where a dismissed workman who is not a member of a trade union makes a claim for reinstatement in his former employment.

JURISDICTION OF THE INDUSTRIAL COURT

The Industrial Court has jurisdiction to deal with the following matters:–

Arbitration of trade disputes

The Court has jurisdiction over trade disputes, existing or apprehended, referred to it for settlement by the Minister of Labour. Trade dispute, as defined in the Industrial Relations Act 1967, means "Any dispute between an employer and his workmen which is connected with the employment or non-employment or the terms of employment or the conditions of work of any such workmen". Trade disputes which fall under this category are rights and interest disputes espoused by trade unions of workmen against employers or trade unions of employers. In other words, these trade disputes involve only organised workers represented by their respective trade unions. (Interest disputes involving unorganised workers arising out of complaints of alleged non-payment of statutory or contractual benefits come under the jurisdiction of the Labour Court discussed earlier. However, rights disputes over dismissals of unorganised workers come under the jurisdiction of the Industrial Court and will be discussed later.

Disputing parties have no direct access to refer any trade dispute to the Industrial Court for arbitration.

Reference may be made under two circumstances. Firstly, a dispute may be referred by the Minister on his own initiative if he is satisfied that it is expedient to do so. This is subject to the proviso that in a trade dispute involving any Government service or the service of any statutory authority, reference cannot be made except with the consent of the Yang di Pertuan Agong or the State Authority, as the case may be. Secondly, a trade dispute may also be referred by the Minister to the Court on the joint request, in writing, of the disputing trade union of workmen and the employer or the trade union of employers. In both circumstances, if there exists an arrangement for the settlement of trade disputes between them, the Minister must not refer the dispute to the Court unless there has been a failure to obtain a settlement through such arrangement, or if, in his opinion, it is unlikely that the dispute will be expeditiously settled through such arrangements. When a trade dispute has been referred to the Industrial Court by the Minister in the proper exercise of his powers, the Court is vested with jurisdiction and is obliged to determine the matter and make its award.

Arbitration of complaints alleging dismissal without just cause or excuse by unorganised workers

The Industrial Relations Act 1967 permits a workman who is not a member of a trade union to seek redress in the event of dismissal which he believes is without just cause or excuse. The workman may within thirty days of such dismissal file a complaint in writing to the Director General of Industrial Relations to be reinstated in his former employment. If the complaint remains unsettled after conciliatory assistance by the Department, the matter is then reported to the Minister who may, if he thinks fit, refer it to the Industrial Court for arbitration. Again, in this type of dispute, the disputing parties have no direct access to the Court. Reference of any dispute to the Court may be done only by the Minister if he is satisfied that it is expedient to do so.

Arbitration of complaints of unfair labour practices

The Industrial Relations Act 1967 sets out certain basic rights of workmen and employers and their trade unions. It also prohibits workmen, employers and their trade unions from doing certain acts, such as anti-trade union activity, victimisation and other unfair labour practices. Any complaint of contravention of such provisions may be lodged in writing to the Director General of Industrial Relations who will then do whatever he considers necessary or expedient to resolve the complaint. If the complaint remains unresolved after intervention by the Director General, the matter has to be reported to the Minister of Labour. He may, if he thinks fit, refer the complaint to the Industrial Court which shall thereupon conduct a hearing and may make such award as may be deemed necessary or appropriate. Reference of these complaints to the Court can only be made at the discretion of the Minister. The disputing parties have no right of direct access to the Court.

Interpretation of awards or collective agreements

An award made by the Industrial Court, or a collective agreement taken cognizence of by the Court, may run into problems of interpretation or implementation. The parties may disagree. Under a provision in the Industrial Relations Act 1967, the problem may be referred back to the Industrial Court for a decision. Such reference may be made either by the Minister on his own initiative or by any party bound by the award or agreement. Therefore, in this case, either party has the option of direct access to the Court. In dealing with these matters, the Court also has the power to vary the terms of an award if it considers it desirable to do so for the purpose solely of removing ambiguity or uncertainty.

Hearing complaints alleging non-compliance with awards or collective agreements

Any trade union of workmen or an individual workman bound by an award of the Industrial Court or a collective agreement which has been taken cognizance of by the Court can lodge a complaint in writing with it against any act of non-compliance with such award or collective agreement. In this case, the aggrieved party can lodge the complaint directly. In dealing with the complaint, the Court is empowered (a) to make an order directing immediate compliance, (b) to make an order directing proper rectification or restitution for any past contravention of any term of the award or collective agreement, and (c) to make an order to vary or set aside, upon special circumstances, any term of the award or collective agreement. Any person who fails to comply with any such order shall be guilty of an offence and shall, on conviction, be liable to a fine not exceeding two thousand ringgit, or to imprisonment for a term not exceeding one year, or to both; and a further fine of five hundred ringgit for every day during which such offence continues.

Taking cognizance of collective agreements

The Industrial Court also has jurisdiction over all collective agreements. Every collective agreement newly entered into must be jointly deposited by the parties with the Registrar of the Industrial Court within one month from the date of agreement. It is the legal duty of the Registrar to bring the agreement to the notice of the Court for its cognizance. On notification, the Court may, in its discretion, take cognizance or refuse to take cognizance if it considers that the agreement does not comply with certain statutory requirements. The Court may also require the parties to amend the agreement to bring it into conformity with statutory requirements. If they refuse to do so the Court may itself amend the agreement in the manner required. A collective agreement which has been taken cognizance of by the Court is deemed an award of the Court. It is therefore legally binding on the parties. On the contrary, a collective agreement which is not taken cognizance of by the Court is not legally binding on the parties.

Punishment for contempt or misbehaviour committed during Court proceedings

The Industrial Court also has jurisdiction over any contempt or misbehaviour committed in its view or presence. The Court may detain the offender in custody or have him removed. The Court may also punish the offender by fine or imprisonment, or discharge him or remit his punishment on his submission to the order of the Court, or on his making an apology to the satisfaction of the Court. There is no appeal from an exercise by the Court of its jurisdiction in this matter.

POWERS OF THE INDUSTRIAL COURT

Although not an ordinary judicial court, the Industrial Court is given some judicial powers. As provided in the Industrial Relations Act 1967, the Court may exercise the following powers: –

– order that any party be joined, substituted or struck off;

– summon before it the parties to the dispute and any other person who in its opinion is connected with the proceedings;

– take evidence on oath or affirmation and compel the production before it of books, papers, documents and things;

– hear and determine the dispute even though a party has failed to submit any written statement within such time as may be prescribed by the President, or in the absence of any party to the dispute who has been served with a notice or summons to appear;

– conduct any of its proceedings or any part of them in private;

– call for the assistance of any experts after consultation with the Minister of Labour;

– generally direct and do all such things as are necessary or expedient for the expeditious determination of the dispute.

Among the powers conferred on the President of the Court is the power to regulate the procedure and proceedings of the Court as he thinks fit and, with the approval of the Minister of Labour, to make rules governing such procedure and proceedings.

REPRESENTATION AT PROCEEDINGS OF THE COURT

In proceedings before the Industrial Court, a party to a dispute may be represented by various people. Where the party is a trade union, it may be represented by an officer or an employee of the trade union. If the party is an employer, he may appear personally or be represented by his duly authorised employee. In the event that he is a member of a trade union of employers, he may be represented by an officer or an employee of such trade union. A workman who is not a member of a trade union may appear personally in proceedings relating to his claim for reinstatement in respect of his dismissal. In all the above cases, an advocate may only appear on their behalf with the permission of the President or Chairman of the Court. It is also possible for a party to be represented by any official of an organisation of employers or workmen registered locally in the country although such organisation is not a registered trade union. For instance, a trade union involved in a dispute before the Court may be represented by an official of the Malaysian Trades Union Congress which is an organisation of workmen registered under the Societies Act. If the status of a representative before the Court is in question, it shall be determined by the President or Chairman of the Court, as the case may be, whose decision is final.

AWARDS OF THE INDUSTRIAL COURT

"Award" refers to a decision of the Industrial Court in respect of any trade dispute or matter referred to it or any decision or order made by it under the

Industrial Relations Act 1967. The Act empowers the Court to make an award, including an interim award, relating to matters referred to it under the relevant provisions. As provided in the Act, the award of the Industrial Court shall be final and conclusive, and shall not be challenged, appealed against, reviewed, quashed or called in question in any court. The effect of this finality or ouster clause has been judicially established. In a recent decision of the Privy Council in South-East Asia Firebricks Co. Ltd. v. Non-Metallic Mineral Manufacturers Employees Union & Others, Lord Fraser, with reference to the grounds of judicial review in relation to Industrial Court awards, stated that "...... if the inferior tribunal has merely made an error of law which does not affect its jurisdiction, and if its decision is not a nullity for such reason such as breach of the rules of natural justice, then the ouster will be effective". It is now settled that an award of the Industrial Court is final and conclusive and is not reviewable by the High Court unless the applicant can establish that the Industrial Court has made a jurisdictional error of law and not a mere error of law. Following the Privy Council's decision in this case, the Federal Court of Malaysia, in another recent case, elaborated on the nature of jurisdictional error. It held that if the Industrial Court had applied their minds to the proper question, had not asked themselves the wrong question, or taken into account matters which should not have concerned them they would not have made an error of law which affected their jurisdiction, and their award would not have been quashed by certiorari. The Privy Council has brought to an end a number of applications, mostly by employers, to the High Court for a writ of certiorari, wanting to quash the awards of the Industrial Court; unless the applications can show on substantial questions of law that the Industrial Court had acted without jurisdiction or had exceeded its jurisdiction.

Although there is no procedure for direct appeal to the High Court against Industrial Court awards, there is a legal procedure to refer questions of law to the High Court. The procedure now is that the applicant should first apply for permission from the Industrial Court. In deciding whether to allow such application, which must be made within thirty days of the relevant award, the Industrial Court must consider the following matters:

- that a question of law has arisen in the course of the proceedings;

- that determination of the question by the Industrial Court has affected has award;

- that in the opinion of the Court, the determination raises sufficient importance to merit reference to the High Court;

- that in the opinion of the Court, the determination raises sufficient doubt to merit reference to the High Court.

The reason for this procedure is to limit applications only to those of merit which are genuinely based on questions of law that are of public interest. Applications should not amount to an appeal on the facts and circumstances of the case. Through such procedure, the settlement of disputes is both expeditious and effective. The parties know quickly where they stand in their relationship in a majority of the cases. This procedure also ensures that Industrial Court awards are not challenged by vexatious applications to the High Court so as to delay the fruits of the awards.

Among the rules laid down in law for the making of an award by the Industrial Court are:

– in the absence of an unanimous decision, the decision is to be taken by a majority of members; in the event of the votes being equal, by the President or Chairman;

– the award should be made without delay and where practicable within thirty days from the date of reference;

– in the case of an award relating to a trade dispute, the Court is required to take into consideration the public interest, the financial implications and the effect of the award on the economy of the country, the industry concerned and the probable effect in related or similar industries;

– the Court is required to act according to equity, good conscience and the substantial merits of the case without regard to technicalities and legal form;

– it may take into consideration any agreement or code relating to employment practices between organisations of employers and workmen respectively where such agreement or code has been approved by the Minister of Labour;

– the award need not be restricted to the specific relief claimed by the parties to the dispute. It may include any matter or thing which the Court thinks necessary or expedient for the purpose of settling the dispute;

– the award may specify the period during which it shall continue in force, and may be retrospective to such date as is specified in the award. However the retrospective date of the award should not be made earlier than 6 months from the date on which the dispute is referred to the Court, except in the following circumstances –

(i) where it is a decision concerning any question relating to interpretation of an award or collective agreement;

(ii) where it is an order, pertaining to non-compliance with an award or collective agreement or an order for the reinstatement of a workman in respect of his dismissal.

– if an agreement is reached between the parties during the proceedings before the Court, the Court in making its award may have regard to the terms of the agreement;

– if an agreement is reached before the Court commences its proceedings, the terms of such agreement may be recorded and adopted.

Any award of the Industrial Court is binding on the following persons:–

– all parties to the dispute;

– any successor, assignee or transferee of any employer or trade union of employers and any successor to any trade union of workmen which is a party to the dispute. Therefore, a new employer who takes over the business of the old employer is bound by an award as a transferee;

– all existing and future workmen employed in the undertaking to which the dispute relates;

– all members of a trade union of employers to whom the dispute relates and to which dispute the trade union is a party, and the successors, assigness or transferees of such members;

– It is an implied term of the contract between the workmen and employers bound by the award that the rates of wages to be paid and the conditions of employment to be observed under the contract will be in accordance with the award unless varied by a subsequent award or agreement between the parties. This may be from the date of the award or as from such date or for such period as may be specified in the award.

FUNCTIONING OF THE INDUSTRIAL COURT

The Industrial Court functions as the uppermost tier of the country's industrial relations system. Thus disputes which remain unresolved by negotiation and conciliation are referred to it for arbitration. The concept of compulsory arbitration embodied in the Industrial Court has through its efficacy and efficiency strengthened the industrial relations system and promoted industrial harmony. Since its inception in 1965, the Court has played an important role in bringing about expeditious settlement of labour disputes. It has thus fulfilled the objectives for which it was established. The awards handed down by the Court usually contain reasons supported by legal authorities for every decision made. This practice has greatly contributed to improved industrial relations by influencing both employers and trade unions to approach issues in a rational manner. In this respect, the Industrial Court supplements the functions of the Industrial Relations Department in promoting cordial and co-operative labour-management relations. Generally, the system is working well.

Established norms have been improved from time to time to ensure fast and speedy disposal of cases. Generally, cases are mentioned within fourteen days of their reference to the Court. This enables early hearing dates. Cases involving interpretation or non-compliance of awards and collective agreements are heard, and decisions handed down within one to two months from the date of reference. A specific Division of the Court deals with disputes pertaining to terms and conditions of employment. These are normally heard and disposed of within two to three months from the date of reference. Other Divisions of the Court handle dismissal cases involving both organised and unorganised workers. These cases are heard and awards handed down, in most cases, within nine to ten months from the date of reference. With the various Divisions of the Court handling specific types of cases, thereby specialising in their respective fields, a satisfactory uniformity and consistency is being developed in the awards.

With the rapid increase in the number of new industries in Malaysia, the size of the country's workforce and the number of trade unions, their membership and their activities have increased rapidly over the years. Consequently, there has been a sharp increase in the number of trade disputes reported to the Industrial Relations Department for conciliation, and a substantial increase in unsettled disputes referred to the Court for arbitration. The 1984 tally of 436 disputes referred to the Court represents a record to date. In 1984, as in previous years, there were more direct reference cases than those referred to the Court by the Minister of Labour. In that year, 219 cases (50.2 per cent) were referred directly to the Court, compared to 217 cases (49.8 per cent) referred to the Court by the Minister.

The Malaysian Industrial Court, besides gaining prominence within the country as well as in neighbouring countries, has also gained increasing acceptance and respect among both sides in industry. This is reflected by the constantly high degree of compliance with its awards, and the high regard the parties have for the Court's impartiality and fairness in dealing with the cases referred to it. So far, during the nineteen years of the Court's existence from 1965 to 1984, out of a total of 2316 awards handed down, only 88 or 3.8 per cent were challenged in the High Court. Out of 57 cases of Writs of Certiorari so far heard and disposed of by the High Court, 30 Industrial Court awards have been upheld 18 awards have been quashed and 9 cases were withdrawn by the parties.

IMPACT OF COMPULSORY ARBITRATION ON COLLECTIVE BARGAINING

Compulsory arbitration was first introduced in 1965 when it covered only trade disputes in the essential services. Subsequently it became a permanent feature of the country's industrial relations system. It has been applied generally to all trade disputes since the promulgation of the Industrial Relations Act in 1967 which also established the present Industrial Court. Prior to 1965, voluntary arbitration prevailed.

In adopting compulsory arbitration, it was evidently not the intention of the government to withdraw its encouragement and support for collective bargaining. Time and experience have shown that free collective bargaining is the most viable and desirable instrument for regulation of wages. The current system has been working very well. Continuous efforts are made to improve and refine it. The government deems it more practical and meaningful to continue this system, which allows adjustment of wages as we go along, rather than to use a wage policy which may well prove too inflexible and therefore unsuitable. The Minister of Labour, while introducing the Industrial Relations Bill in Parliament in 1967, which led to the introduction of the Industrial Relations Act currently in force said inter alia, ". . . . . the Bill seeks to continue to encourage self-government in industry and it contains a number of provisions not only to safeguard the legitimate rights and interests of workers and employers and their trade unions, but also to ensure the speedy and just settlement of industrial disputes, so that the ever-present public and national interests are not prejudiced while the parties promote their particular interests". In a nutshell, this is the underlying objective and rationale for introducing compulsory arbitration in Malaysia.

Within the context of ILO Conventions No. 87 (Freedom of Association and Protection of the Right to Organise) and No. 98 (Right to Organise and Collective Bargaining), compulsory arbitration applied generally to all disputes may be viewed as having a tendency to undermine or impair collective bargaining in that it takes away the strike weapon from the workers. However, this general view is not necessarily true everywhere and in all situations. In the Malaysian situation, time and experience have shown that compulsory arbitration, as practised now, although it curtails to a certain extent the workers' right to strike, does not undermine, impair or discourage collective bargaining. The Industrial Relations Act 1967, besides requiring compulsory arbitration of disputes which cannot be resolved voluntarily by the parties, also promotes and facilitates collective bargaining. It does this by providing an adequate legal framework to ensure observance of basic rules and practices in "good faith bargaining" by the parties. A certain degree of voluntarism is still retained in the Malaysian compulsory arbitration system in that there are procedures in law for the voluntary reference of trade disputes to the Industrial Court on the joint application of both parties. The system of compulsory arbitration in Malaysia has been evolved and adapted to suit the overall interests of the nation. Two decades of experience have shown that the system does not undermine or suppress collective bargaining. The system has been effective in moderating the conduct of both sides in dealing with each other. This, coupled with their increasing maturity has contributed to the growth of collective bargaining. Collective bargaining in this country is gradually expanding as reflected by the increasing number of collective agreements freely entered into during the past few years as shown below :–

Year	No. of Collective Agreements entered into and taken cognizance of by the Industrial Court
1980	207
1981	262
1982	266
1983	268
1984	234
1985	330

Based on the average over the past ten years, 85 per cent of collective agreement negotiations were freely and voluntarily settled through direct negotiation or conciliation. Only 15 per cent ended in deadlock necessitating reference to arbitration for settlement. Again, about 40 per cent of the deadlocked cases were freely and voluntarily referred to the Industrial Court. Only 60 per cent were referred to the Court through compulsory procedures. These figures indicate clearly that, with compulsory arbitration, there has been no suppression of free collective bargaining in Malaysia.

CONCEPTS AND PRINCIPLES CONTRIBUTING TO THE SUCCESS OF THE SYSTEM

Malaysia's success in compulsory arbitration did not come easily. It developed from painstaking efforts to improve and refine the system in the light of experience gained over time. Some significant concepts and principles which have been applied to the system and which have shaped its present characteristic features constitute a major factor in its success.

In making an award, the Industrial Court is governed by the principle that it is to act according to equity, good conscience and the substantial merits of the case without regard to technicalities and legal form. This enables the Court to also take non-legal matters into consideration when making its award; viz. the public interest, the financial implications and the effect of the award on the economy of the country and on the industry concerned, and also the probable effect on related or similar industries. Furthermore, the Court need not restrict its award to the specific relief claimed by the parties. In this respect it is empowered to include any matter which it thinks necessary or expedient for the purpose of settling the dispute. Thus, the Court's jurisdiction is adequately flexible and is not restricted as in an ordinary court which must always decide according to law. In making its award, the main concern is not only the dispensation of social justice so as to ensure peace and harmony in industrial relations, but also the promotion of a climate conducive to economic development through private investment.

The underlying concept with regard to reference of disputes to compulsory arbitration is that the Industrial Court is to function as a court of last resort. Arbitration should, as a rule, be resorted to only after every voluntary means of resolving the dispute has been tried without success. This promotes the concept of self-government in industry and preserves the fundamental role of negotiation and collective bargaining as the chief method of dispute settlement.

Industrial Court awards cannot be challenged, appealed against, reviewed, quashed or called in question in any court. This reflects the concept that the Court's award on any trade dispute is final and conclusive unless the Court has acted in excess or in want of jurisdiction. In such a case, the award may be reviewed and quashed by the High Court through writ of certiorari. This concept has had the desirable effect of bringing about expeditious and effective settlement of trade disputes. It has helped to ensure that the Court's awards are not challenged by vexatious appeals to the High Court so as to delay the fruits of the awards.

CONCLUSION

One of the main objectives of the Malaysian government's labour policy is to provide as simple and inexpensive a machinery as is practicable for the quick settlement of these disputes between employers and workers which they themselves are unable to resolve voluntarily. The existing Industrial Court has been functioning effectively to fulfill the desired objective. Now, twenty years after its inception, the Court has become recognised as a critical ingredient in the success of the country's industrial relations system. It has, without doubt, won acceptance, and will continue to win an ever greater measure of acceptance, from both employers and workers, whether unionised or not. Through its awards, the Industrial Court has laid down fairly clear rules of natural justice in the excercise of managerial rights by employers. It has also laid down procedures for inquiries into alleged misconduct of workers to prevent such exercise of managerial rights by employers in circumstances which could be deemed to be done in bad faith. While recognising employers' common law rights to hire and fire, to promote, transfer and to discipline their workers, the Court through its awards has helped to mellow the exercise of these rights by enunciating principles and guidelines of good conscience. Its awards have from time to time laid down broad limits to trade union claims and negotiations in regard to terms and conditions of employment. By the persuasive authority of these awards, settlement of claims through direct negotiations and through conciliation have become speedier, thereby avoiding unnecessary waste of time, money, energy and emotional friction. By the ready availability of its dispute settlement machinery, it has helped to avoid a substantial number of strikes and lock-outs, and the loss of man-days in consequence.

The system of arbitration of trade disputes in Malaysia is not perfect but it has withstood the test of time. It will continue to grow and develop to keep abreast of developments in industrial relations and to meet the ever-changing needs of a fast developing nation.

APPENDIX 'A'

CASES REFERRED TO THE INDUSTRIAL COURT
1980 – JUNE 1985

	1980	*1981*	*1982*	*1983*	*1984*	*1985 Jan-Jun*
No. of cases brought forward from previous year:	194	177	140	79	100	147
No. of cases referred during the year:	197	253	240	355	436	201
Total No. of cases for hearing:	391	430	380	434	536	348

APPENDIX 'B'

BREAKDOWN OF CASES REFERRED BY NATURE OF DISPUTES

Nature of Disputes	*No. of Cases*											
	1980	*%*	*1981*	*%*	*1982*	*%*	*1983*	*%*	*1984*	*%*	*1985 Jan-Jun*	*%*
A. References by Minister:												
(i) Terms & conditions of employment:	29	14.7	39	15.4	43	17.9	47	13.2	60	13.3	30	15.0
(ii) Dismissal of unionised workers	58	29.4	50	19.8	28	11.7	45	12.7	65	14.9	31	15.4
(iii) Dismissal of non-unionised workers	49	24.9	50	19.8	47	19.6	79	22.3	92	21.1	65	32.3
Sub-total:	136	69.0	139	55.0	118	49.2	171	48.2	217	49.8	126	62.7
B. References direct to Court:												
(i) Non-compliance, interpretation & variation of award:	26	13.2	57	22.5	67	27.9	60	17.5	116	26.6	27	13.4
(ii) Non-compliance & interpretation of collective agreements:	22	11.2	36	14.2	34	14.2	69	19.4	74	17.0	29	14.4
(iii) Others (amendment to collective agreements, cost etc.)	8	4.1	1	0.4	2	0.8	34	0.6	12	2.7	4	2.0
(iv) Application for reference to High Court on questions of law:	5	2.5	20	7.9	19	7.9	19	5.3	17	3.9	15	7.5
Sub-total	61	31.0	114	45.0	122	50.8	184	51.8	219	50.2	75	37.3
Grand total:	197	100%	253	100%	240	100%	355	100%	436	100%	201	100%

APPENDIX 'C'

NUMBER OF CASES SETTLED

	1980	%	*1981*	%	*1982*	%	*1983*	%	*1984*	%	*1985 Jan-Jun*	%
No. of awards handed down	164	76.6	237	79.3	258	85.4	291	86.4	298	76.4	123	75.9
No. of cases settled out of Court after being referred:	50	23.4	62	20.7	44	14.6	46	13.6	91	23.6	39	24.1
Total	214	100%	299	100%	302	100%	337	100%	389	100%	162	100%

APPENDIX 'D'

AWARDS BROUGHT BEFORE THE HIGH COURT

		Total June 1965 to June 84	*1984 Jan-June*	*1983*	*1982*	*1981*	*1980*	*1979*	*1978*	*1977*	*1965 to 1976*
(i)	Total no. of awards handed down	2,316	298	291	258	237	164	181	185	143	559
(ii)	No. of awards challenged in High Court:	88	7	3	4	3	6	14	15	9	27
	% of (i)	3.8%	2.3%	1.0%	1.6%	1.3%	3.7%	7.7%	8.1%	6.3%	4.8%
(iii)	No. of cases pending decision from High Court:	31	7	2	1	2	2	7	2	2	6
	% of (ii)	35.2%	100%	66.7%	25%	66.7%	33.3%	50.0%	13.3%	22.2%	22.2%
(iv)	No. of cases disposed off:	57	0	1	3	1	4	7	13	7	21
(v)	No. of awards upheld	30	0	1	2	1	3	2	6	3	12
	% of (iv)	52.6%	–	100%	66.7%	100%	75%	28.6%	46.2%	42.9%	57.1%
(vi)	No. of awards quashed	18	0	0	1	0	0	3	5	4	5
	% of (iv)	31.6%	–	–	33.3%	–	–	42.9%	50.0%	57.1%	23.8%
(vii)	No. of cases settled or withdrawn:	9	0	0	0	0	1	2	2	0	4
	% of (iv)	15.8%	–	–	–	–	25%	28.6%	20.0%	–	19.1%

VOLUNTARY AND COMPULSORY ARBITRATION OF LABOUR DISPUTES IN THE PHILIPPINES

by

Carmelo C. Noriel,
Deputy Labour Minister of the Philippines.

STATE POLICY ON ARBITRATION

The State policy on labour arbitration in the Philippines is embodied in the "protection to labour clause" of the Philippine Constitution of 1973. This clause or provision of the Constitution refers among other things, to the right to self-organisation and collective bargaining and the authority of the State *to provide for compulsory arbitration.* The Labour Code of the Philippines of 1974 in turn declares it to be the policy of the government to promote free collective bargaining *including voluntary arbitration* and to provide adequate administrative machinery for the expeditious settlement of labour disputes. The government machinery for labour dispute settlement consists essentially of conciliation, mediation and compulsory arbitration.

Under the existing State policy and law, the centrepiece of labour relations remains collective bargaining in its broadest sense. Collective bargaining as such is used as a process to fix terms and conditions of employment generally through the conclusion of collective agreements and as a mode of dispute settlement.

It is inherent in a collective bargaining set-up to consider direct or bilateral negotiations between the parties as the most preferred mode of thrashing out differences and problems. Self-reliance and self-determination of the social partners should be the foundation of sound labour relations. So are independence and voluntariness. This is what collective bargaining is all about. Should such negotiations fail, it is consistent with collective bargaining to encourage the adoption by the parties of agreed methods to settle their disputes in which the parties themselves continue to be in full control. What is important is that they are jointly selecting, freely and voluntarily, the mode of their choice. An example of such selection is the establishment of a grievance machinery leading to voluntary arbitration under which the collective agreement is deemed to be an extension of the collective bargaining process.

In cases, however, where government intervention is required or necessary, the most preferred mode of settling labour disputes is conciliation and mediation in which a conciliator is called upon merely to assist the parties in the settlement of their dispute. He does not order or compel the parties to accept his will or decision. The end result is still agreement between the parties. In the absence of an agreement concerning certain issues, specially on rights disputes, the use of compulsory arbitration as a recourse of last resort can be considered. If it is to be effective, however, it must not compete with or substitute for collective bargaining. It must be independent, impartial and just. This is how voluntary and compulsory arbitration are perceived to operate within the context of the labour relations system in the Philippines.

VOLUNTARY ARBITRATION SYSTEM

THE LAW

R.A. 875

Voluntary arbitration was formally introduced in principle in the Philippines with the advent of free collective bargaining under Republic Act No. 875 of 1953 otherwise known as the "Industrial Peace Act". The law formally encouraged the establishment of a "machinery for the adjustment of grievances, including any question that may arise from the application or interpretation of the collective bargaining agreement". It was perhaps due to the influence of the successful experience with voluntary arbitration in a number of industrialised countries, notably the United States, that many if not all collective agreements in the Philippines eventually contained provisions for grievance handling with voluntary arbitration as the last step. In the initial years after the passage of R.A. 875, however, there were not enough employers and labour unions with effective grievance machinery which placed voluntary arbitration as the terminal step. A separate Private Arbitration Law, Republic Act No. 876, was passed also in 1953 but with a provision in Section 3 thereof that "it shall not apply to controversies and cases which are subject to the jurisdiction of the Court of Industrial Relations". The Act applies primarily to arbitration of civil cases and controversies.

P.D. 21

It was in 1972, under Presidential Decree No. 21, when a serious attempt was made to institutionalise voluntary arbitration as a distinct and separate mode of labour dispute settlement. The Decree created an ad hoc National Labour Relations Commission with power to conciliate, mediate and arbitrate all types of labour-management disputes.

With respect to voluntary arbitration, Sec. 3 of P.D. 21 provided that the parties to any dispute, grievance or issue shall first exhaust all steps in the grievance procedure provided for in the applicable collective bargaining agreement, or such other means of dispute settlement mutually agreed upon by them before either or both parties may raise an issue, dispute or grievance to the Commission. The Commission shall require the complaining party to show proofs of failure to settle the issue, dispute or grievance under the procedure agreed upon by them before assuming jurisdiction.

Section 4 of the Decree provides further that before assuming jurisdiction over the case, the Commission or its duly authorised representative shall give the parties a chance to submit their problem for voluntary arbitration. However, if the parties fail to agree on the arbitrator, the Commission may designate an arbitrator to hear and decide such grievance dispute or issue or itself act as the arbitrator.

Section 6 of the same Decree requires that all collective bargaining agreements shall contain a provision designating a voluntary arbitrator who may be an individual or a committee, to decide all disputes and grievances arising out of the implementation of the collective bargaining agreement. All existing agreements without such provision shall be duly amended to include such provision and such amendment shall be reported immediately to the Commission. It was this mandatory character of the law that gave rise to what has been termed, since then, as "mandatory voluntary arbitration".

The changed political situation under the emergency rule of 1972 helped to provide the momentum for the speedy disposition of labour cases. Thousands of cases were disposed of with dispatch, the great majority of which were resolved through voluntary arbitration.

Labour Code of 1974

Because of the experience under Presidential Decree 21 indicating the effectiveness and usefulness of voluntary arbitration, the government did not find any reason to depart from its policy and law on labour arbitration. In 1974, the Labour Code was promulgated and Article 211 in the Declaration of Policy provided that it is the policy of the State to promote, among others, free collective bargaining including voluntary arbitration as a mode of settling labour disputes or industrial disputes.

The Labour Code, before it was amended by Presidential Decree 850 (1975), allowed a much broader scope and coverage of disputes subject to voluntary arbitration. All questions arising from the interpretation and implementation of collective agreements, including all cases involving disciplinary actions and termination cases of workers covered by collective agreements, fall under the original and exclusive jurisdiction of voluntary arbitrators.

It is required under the Code that the parties to a collective agreement shall include in it provisions to ensure mutual observance of the terms and conditions of the agreement and to establish a machinery for the adjustment of grievances. Article 261 added that all disputes, grievances or matters arising from the implementation or interpretation of a collective bargaining agreement shall be thrashed out in accordance with the grievance procedure provided for by such agreement. Under Art. 262 disputes, grievances or matters not settled through the grievance procedure shall be referred to and decided or settled through the prescribed voluntary arbitration procedure in the collective bargaining agreement.

The Code also requires that every collective bargaining agreement shall designate in advance an arbitrator or panel of arbitrators or include a provision making the selection of such arbitrator or panel of arbitrators definite and certain when the need arises. Such arbitrator or panel of arbitrators shall have exclusive and original jurisdiction to settle or decide all disputes, grievances and matters arising from the implementation or interpretation of a collective bargaining agreement after going through the grievance procedure. The law mandates the Labour Arbiter or the Bureau of Labour Relations not to entertain such disputes, grievances and matters and that voluntary arbitration awards or decisions shall be final, inappealable and executory.

Implementing Rules

Rule XI of the Implementing Rules of the Labour Code specifies the procedure on voluntary arbitration. It defines the exclusive and original jurisdiction of a voluntary arbitrator in Section 1 thereof as follows: "The voluntary arbitrator or panel of voluntary arbitrators named in the collective agreement or selected by the parties shall have exclusive and original jurisdiction to settle or decide all disputes, grievances or matters arising from the implementation or interpretation of collective agreements which have gone through the grievance procedure. The Labour Arbiter or the Bureau shall not entertain such disputes, grievances or matters."

According to Section 2 of the Rules, disputes, grievances or other matters arising from the interpretation or implementation of a collective agreement filed with the Labour Arbiter or the Bureau of the Labour Relations Division shall be dismissed immediately and referred to the voluntary arbitrator or voluntary arbitrators named in the collective agreement or selected by the parties, for resolution.

Section 3 of the Rules reiterates the policy of the State on voluntary arbitration of all labour-management disputes and provides that any case filed with the Labour Relations Division, Labour Arbiters and compulsory arbitrators may be referred for voluntary arbitration at any time before submission of the case for decision.

Voluntary Arbitration Awards

Section 4 emphasizes the final and inappealable character of voluntary arbitration awards and decisions. Such decisions or awards may be executed when any interested party files a motion for execution before the Labour Arbiter in the Regional Office where the interested party resides, upon which the Labour Arbiter shall issue a writ of execution requiring the sheriff or the proper officer to execute the voluntary arbitration award or decision.

Section 5 provides for exception to the finality of voluntary arbitration awards and decisions. Thus, except in cases where the parties agree that the voluntary arbitration decision shall be final and executory, or after they have had a choice not to submit to voluntary arbitration but have opted for the same, voluntary arbitration decisions or awards on money claims involving more than P100,000.00 or 40 per cent of the paid-up capital of the respondent employer, whichever is lower, may be appealed to the National Labour Relations Commission; but only on grounds of (a) abuse of discretion; and (b) gross incompetence.

The appealing party shall, within ten (10) days upon receipt of such decision or awards, file his appeal to the voluntary arbitrator or panel of arbitrators stating specifically the grounds therefor, the errors committed and the relief sought. The appealing party shall serve a copy of the appeal on the appellee who shall in turn file his answer within ten (10) days from receipt thereof.

The Commission shall decide the appeal within twenty (20) working days from receipt of the entire records of the case. The voluntary arbitrator or panel of voluntary arbitrators shall forward the entire records of the case to the Commission within five (5) days from receipt of the appelee's answer.

Before the Labour Code amendments introduced under Batas Pambansa Blg. 130 and its implementing rules, promulgated in 1981, it was required that to qualify for certification, collective agreements shall include provisions establishing an adequate grievance and voluntary arbitration machinery including an arbitration clause that will ensure the selection of a voluntary arbitrator or panel of arbitrators to settle and decide problems arising from the interpretation and application of the collective agreement.

TERMINATION CASES AND VOLUNTARY ARBITRATION

In 1975, PD 850 was promulgated transferring the jurisdiction over termination cases to the Regional Directors and removing from the original and exclusive jurisdiction of the grievance machinery and voluntary arbitrators, termination cases in companies where there are existing collective bargaining agreements. The reasons for the transfer were stated in Policy Instructions No. 14 which was promulgated to clarify the issue of jurisdiction. It states:

"Under the unrevised Labour Code, termination cases where there was a CBA were placed under the grievance machinery and voluntary arbitration for the following reasons: 1) to relieve the newly-established backlogloaded NLRC of some cases, 2) to test the capacity of unions to protect their own members in termination cases, and 3) to create a demand for voluntary arbitration. This Department and some labour leaders were originally opposed to the idea. They were for retaining the system under Presidential Decree No. 21 where the Secretary of Labour had jurisdiction over all termination cases, with or without CBA. However, the DOL Legislative Committee argued strongly for the transfer, in view of which the leadership of the Department of Labour gave it a sixmonth trial period. After more than a year, the experiment has been found ineffective, largely because of the failure of many unions to protect their members through the grievance machinery and voluntary arbitration."

In 1977, Policy Instructions No. 28 was issued to clarify the effect of PD 850 on the policy towards voluntary arbitration insofar as cases involving disciplinary actions of employees covered by collective agreements was concerned. On termination cases, the Policy Instructions stated that in cases where an opposition to an application for clearance to terminate or suspend an employee is filed and the Regional Director finds that the nature of the case does not suit summary investigation, or intricate questions of law are involved, Regional Directors are urged to encourage the parties to submit their cases to a voluntary arbitrator who shall decide the same on the merits based on the agreement of the parties; which agreement shall also indicate the binding effect of the awards. The Regional Director shall certify the case to the Labour Arbiter if the parties indicate their preference for this mode of settlement, or if they refuse or are unable to submit their case to voluntary arbitration.

The same Policy Instructions reiterated the government's commitment to give full support to voluntary arbitration by providing that even interest disputes may be submitted to voluntary arbitration. Thus, in cases of deadlocks in collective bargaining on economic issues where conciliation has failed, the parties may submit their cases to a voluntary arbitrator whose decision shall be final, binding and inappealable if expressly and clearly so indicated in the agreement of the parties, including those involving an amount in excess of P100,000.00 or 40 per cent of the paid-up capital of the respondent employer. All other disputes, grievances or matters affecting the relationship between labour and management or among employees themselves, may be brought by agreement of the parties to voluntary arbitration.

In 1980, another amendatory Decree was passed, Presidential Decree 1691, providing that all disputes, grievances or matters arising from the implementation or interpretation of collective bargaining agreements, including all matters concerning disciplinary action imposed or to be imposed on members of the contracting union, shall be thrashed out in accordance with the grievance procedure provided in such agreement. Where there is no collective bargaining agreement and in cases where the grievance procedure as provided therein does not apply, all such matters should be subject to conciliation and arbitration as provided elsewhere in the Code. The Decree failed to restore clearly the exclusive and original jurisdiction of voluntary arbitrators over termination cases which at that time constituted the majority of voluntary arbitration cases.

As earlier mentioned, amendments to the Labour Code were introduced under Batas Pambansa Blg. 130 which was promulgated into law on 21 August 1981. Batas Pambansa Blg. 130 eliminated the certification requirement for collective bargaining agreements and along with it the mandatory requirement that collective agreements shall include provisions establishing an adequate grievance and voluntary arbitration machinery, including an arbitration clause that will ensure the selection of a voluntary arbitrator or panel of arbitrators, to settle and decide problems arising from the interpretation and application of the collective agreement.

THE STATE OF VOLUNTARY ARBITRATION

An honest assessment of the current state of voluntary arbitration, despite its merits, presents a gloomy situation as far as its acceptance, usefulness and effectiveness as a preferred mode of labour dispute settlement is concerned. In 1979, when the Bureau of Labour Relations was still active in monitoring the progress of voluntary arbitration, it was reported to have compiled only a total of 229 voluntary arbitration awards since the promulgation of the Labour Code in November 1974.

The submission of copies of awards was in response to requests addressed to some 202 voluntary arbitrators accredited under Department Order No. 12 by the Secretary of Labour. It is possible that some arbitrators may have chosen to ignore such requests and there may be cases that were handled by non-listed arbitrators. Since then, hardly a single award or decision by voluntary arbitrators has been filed and submitted to the Bureau.

The Bureau, however, was quoted as having reported in 1978, that based on one study, the cases that were brought to voluntary arbitration represented only 3 per cent of the total arbitrable cases handled by the entire Ministry of Labour and Employment during a given year. At that time the total case load was at least ten thousand a year. The observation made by the Bureau seems to find support in statements made by labour relations practitioners based on their own experience.

One lawyer, for example, who is an accredited voluntary arbitrator and who works for large companies like the Philippine Airlines (PAL) and the Atlantic Gulf and Pacific Company (AG & P), stated on one occasion in 1980, that in the case of PAL, out of hundreds of labour cases, voluntary arbitration was resorted to in only three (3) cases. The same situation obtained in AG & P where, for seven years, only three (3) cases were submitted by the parties to voluntary arbitration. He expressed the view that the situation would be pretty much the same in other companies.

FACTORS AFFECTING VOLUNTARY ARBITRATION

For voluntary arbitration to succeed, it is indeed a requirement that certain "given" factors should be present in the labour relations system. These are:

– a government that is willing to leave the settlement of such disputes to procedures decided upon by the parties themselves, and

– strong unions able to assist individual workers or groups of workers in pursuing their cases and in equally sharing the costs of the proceedings with the employer.

Law and policy issues

Some quarters have noted a sharp decline in cases brought to voluntary arbitration, allegedly due to active government intervention in labour-management relations as reflected in the series of amendments in the law and policy. These effectively discouraged the use of voluntary arbitration in favour of compulsory arbitration and summary proceedings in the Labour Ministry. It is also claimed that the government has been wanting in effectively promoting the use of voluntary arbitration, and that the policies are not clear, or the implementation of law and policies run counter to the declared objectives.

One voluntary arbitrator considers the government attitude as "schizophrenic" especially when it declared the ineffectiveness of voluntary arbitration insofar as termination cases are concerned under Policy Instruction No. 14. It is claimed that by their own official actions, government belied their avowals of voluntary arbitration as a desirable mode of labour dispute settlement. It is said that voluntary arbitration is institutionalised only in law but not in implementation. Preference to voluntary arbitration, they insist, should be given substance and not only lip service. Under such an unfavourable policy and legal framework, they claim that voluntary arbitration is unlikely to succeed. Instead of extensive government intervention, there should be willingness on the part of the State to leave the settlement of labour disputes to the parties themselves.

Trade Union Problems

The need for strong trade unions need not be overemphasized. There can be no effective negotiations concerning terms and conditions of employment in collective bargaining without strong workers' organisations. Such negotiations cannot result in meaningful and mutually satisfactory agreements if there is a great imbalance in the bargaining strengths between employers and employees and their unions.

The current statistics on labour relations may indicate some important factors which may have direct relevance to the state of labour relations in general. Out of a total workforce of 21,643 million, some 9,113 million fall within the category of wage and salary earners. Organised labour, however, claims only a total membership of around 2,119 million representing 23.3 per cent of total salary earners or only 10 per cent of the entire labour force. Moreover, they are organized into some 2,331 registered trade unions, 128 federations and 7 trade union centres. Rampant union-raiding and inter-union conflicts indicate a heavy concentration on the already organised sector to the prejudice of the millions of workers who are yet to be organised.

The problem of intense inter and intra-union rivalry may also be reflected in the number of collective agreements which unions have concluded on behalf of their members. There are at present a total of 2,415 collective agreements filed with the Bureau of Labour Relations covering about 328,000 workers or only 3.6 per cent of the total wage and salary workforce. The quality of collective agreements is another aspect that has to be looked into even as trade union groups continue to raise the alleged proliferation of "yellow dog contracts" or "sweetheart" agreements entered into by some parties.

Problem of delays

There are complaints relating to delays in voluntary arbitration proceedings. One study conducted in 1979 by a voluntary arbitrator places the length of time needed by arbitrators to dispose of their cases as ranging from one month to thirty-six months. Another study indicates that delays are generally attributable to frequent requests for postponement by either party, the time needed to prepare decisions and other legal technicalities. It is pointed out that because of excessive legalism and the dominance of lawyers, all the problems experienced in compulsory arbitration under Commonwealth Act. No. 130 and Republic Act No. 875 are likewise encountered in voluntary arbitration.

Qualification of voluntary arbitrators

Other questions pertain to the impartiality and competence of some arbitrators. Arbitrators, they say, are either known as a management man or a labour man. In cases where lawyers act as arbitrators, it is claimed that the decisions do not take into account factors of productivity in terms of costs, revenues and output – which have a greater impact on the general economy and which in the view of some sectors, should override the narrow interests of labour.

It was also pointed out that we lack professional arbitrators, unlike in the United States. Arbitrators' associations do not appear to be fully committed to their objectives. Members of the Arbitrators Association of the Philippines (AAP) and the Philippine (Association) of Professional Arbitrators (PAPA), are often described as part-time or spare time arbitrators. Questions have been raised as to what they need to accomplish to professionalise their ranks, to attract more clients and to upgrade their technical skills. Aside from acquiring technical skills through continuous training, arbitrators need to be exposed to trends, practices and developments in the area of labour relations in general, and collective bargaining in particular, and to be able to reflect such trends and practices in the decisions that they hand down.

In another study conducted to determine, among other things, the preference of parties in resolving their disputes, a question was asked on who they think is most capable of deciding their disputes fairly. Both labour and management practitioners answered that retired judges were the most honest and most trusted arbitrators followed by professors, incumbent judges, government officials and businessmen. On one occasion, it was pointed out by a management representative that in a number of collective agreements, a former Director of the UP Law Centre, a lady lawyer and professor, is named as the voluntary arbitrator. If she is not available, she is given by the parties the authority to name her own representative. This speaks of the high esteem and regard which the parties have for the professor. Such an arbitrator could be one of the few who, because of her competence and impartiality, has earned the trust and confidence of the parties.

Cost of arbitration and other cultural factors

Another reservation, coming mostly from representatives of trade unions, pertains to the cost of arbitration – the fees of arbitrators and other incidental expenses which can be a drain on union finances. Another factor cited relates to the cultural framework in which labour-management relations has been made to operate. This refers to the years of "conditioning" to compulsory arbitration, marked by heavy emphasis on adjudication through industrial courts and tribunals which may have influenced two or three generations of workers and management who are prone to settle their disputes with the help of lawyers and a judge or arbiter.

There is also the cultural trait to rely on a government official or third party on whom they can place the blame should the case be a losing proposition. Such trait is also promoted in compulsory arbitration because of the availability of the right to appeal, thus providing another excuse for losing. This is true in some cases in voluntary arbitration.

RECOMMENDATIONS

General

Based on the foregoing discussions and observations, the following general recommendations may be considered to help renew the faith and commitment of all concerned to the merits of voluntary arbitration:

– Government, workers and employers must share in the commitment, faith and respect for a labour relations system which is principally based on collective bargaining of which voluntary arbitration is very much a part.

– There should be a sharing too, in the commitment to develop strong organisations of workers and employers which constitute the foundation of a labour relations system which recognises and respects the rights to organise and collective bargaining. Without such free, strong and independent organisations, the system itself will always prove to be inadequate if not a failure. In such a situation, voluntary arbitration cannot prosper.

– It should be a clear policy of government consistent with the principles of collective bargaining to promote free, direct and voluntary negotiations between workers' and employers' representatives concerning terms and conditions of employment. This should include the use of voluntary arbitration as a last step and other agreed methods of dispute settlement. If this is not clear, this should be clarified and reaffirmed. Government intervention should in principle be made available but utilised only upon request of the parties except in very limited cases such as those involving the national interest or violations of law.

– There should be a shared belief by all those engaged in dispute settlement that the ultimate goal is the just, speedy and expeditious resolution of disputes in order to ensure industrial peace and social justice. There is presently an enormous number of labour disputes which can be handled effectively only if all the mechanisms available are working efficiently and well. The mechanisms include the entire scope of bilateral negotiations, voluntary arbitration, conciliation and mediation as well as compulsory arbitration.

– As a mode of dispute settlement, voluntary arbitration must prove itself as a distinct, effective and superior alternative to other means of resolving disputes. Efforts should be made therefore to make it different, to be superior, to be more advantageous from the point of view of the parties themselves. Otherwise if there is no difference or advantage at all compared to other available means, the parties to a case are not likely to opt for voluntary arbitration.

– Voluntary arbitrators should win the trust, the confidence and respect of the parties by providing a just, speedy and inexpensive means of settling differences between workers and employers. In the same vein, the approach and procedure in voluntary arbitration should be a better alternative, for instance, to compulsory arbitration.

– Continuous training and exposure of labour arbitrators to the many facets of labour relations should be emphasised. Government may lead in this programme but the support of trade unions and employers, arbitration associations, private institutions and universities is essential.

– There should be a continuing exchange of views on the different aspects of voluntary arbitration through training programmes and seminars supported and participated in by all sectors in the field of industrial relations including voluntary arbitrators. Regular publications on concepts, developments and trends here and in other countries must also be encouraged.

– The effective use of the grievance machinery with voluntary arbitration as the last step must be strongly promoted under a mandatory scheme if necessary, or as an interim measure in order to develop self-reliance and self-government in the collective relationship.

– The thrust of the labour relations policy should be focused at the shopfloor or the enterprise level which actually provides the base for the development of strong organisations of workers and where voluntary arbitration itself can be of utmost importance and usefulness.

Specific

In the Forum on Arbitration held on 20 February 1985 at the Manila Hilton under the sponsorship of the Ministry of Labour and Employment, the following specific recommendations were adopted with respect to voluntary arbitration.

Jurisdiction (a) The jurisdiction of voluntary and compulsory arbitration should be clearly distinguished and delineated. To strengthen voluntary arbitration and make (through load-reduction) the machinery of compulsory arbitration more effective, the concurrent jurisdiction enjoyed by labour arbiters and voluntary arbitrators over disputes due to unfair labour practices and money claims when they arise from interpretation or implementation of collective bargaining agreements should be resolved. The original and exclusive jurisdiction over such cases should be clearly granted to voluntary arbitrators.

(b) The jurisdictional competence should be reflected by law and strictly enforced, so that labour arbiters and the Bureau of Labour Relations should have power to dismiss cases properly under the jurisdiction of the enterprise level grievance machinery and of the voluntary arbitrators.

(c) Disputes that should be resolved through voluntary arbitration are those arising from the interpretation or implementation of a collective bargaining agreement. Some labour representatives argued however that the law should not compel parties to use voluntary arbitration.

Cost of Voluntary Arbitration (a) Arbitration fees should be standardised at a reasonable or affordable level. A labour representative noted, however, that voluntary arbitration, based on his own experience, is not costly.

Selecting qualified voluntary arbitrators (a) The Employers' Confederation of the Philippines, the unions, and the Arbitration Association of the Philippines should draw-up a list of voluntary arbitrators who will then be accredited by the NLRC. Only those in the list will be allowed to arbitrate cases.

(b) At the enterprise level, the choice of voluntary arbitrator in a particular dispute shall be done through the submission of fifteen (15) names from among those listed by each of the employer and the union. The commonly selected arbitrator shall be chosen by drawing, through lottery, of a name from those not previously nominated.

Programmes supportive of voluntary arbitration (a) Create a body or unit within the present National Labour Relations Commission (NLRC) to promote the practice of voluntary arbitration. The unit shall compile names of qualified voluntary arbitrators and accredit the same. The Unit shall also develop a procedure for fairly determining how voluntary arbitrators may be assigned to handle specific cases.

(b) Conduct regular educational programmes, seminars, symposia, and provide fora to encourage management and labour sectors to use voluntary arbitration as a preferred mode of dispute settlement.

CONCLUSIONS

It is submitted that voluntary arbitration in the Philippines continues to have great prospects as an effective mode of labour dispute settlement, particularly in line with the announced government position exhorting workers and employers to make use of all voluntary and peaceful methods of settling labour-management disputes and for the government to exercise "least intervention" in labour dispute resolution. Finally, the use of voluntary arbitration is in consonance with the provision of the proposed 1986 Constitution of the Philippines which seeks to promote "the preferential use of voluntary modes in settling disputes, including conciliation, and shall enforce their mutual compliance therewith to foster industrial peace."

In line with the new policy and the Constitutional mandate and in accordance with the guiding principles set by the Presidential Commission on Government Reorganization, the Labour Ministry is now undertaking a ministry-wide restructuring of its organizations and functions to reflect its critical role in the national economic recovery programme. To emphasise the new labour relations thrust of the government, a National Labour Conciliation and Mediation

Board is being proposed to be created to handle primarily the preventive conciliation, mediation and voluntary arbitration functions of the Labour Ministry. The Board shall be composed of an Administrator, two (2) Deputy Administrators to be appointed by the President upon recommendation of the Minister of Labour from among persons outstanding in the field of labour. There shall be as many Conciliators-Mediators as the needs of the public service requires who shall have at least three (3) years experience in labour relations and who shall be appointed by the Minister of Labour upon the recommendation of the Administrator. The Administrator, Deputy Administrators and Conciliators-Mediators shall receive the same salary as the Chairman, Commissioners and Labour Arbiters of the NLAC, respectively. The Board shall have its main office in Metro Manila and shall establish regional branches to be headed by Executive Conciliators-Mediators.

COMPULSORY ARBITRATION SYSTEM

Labour arbitration in the Philippines is exercised by several agencies with the National Labour Relations Commission (NLRC) as the major arbitration arm of the Ministry. The other agencies are the Bureau of Labour Relations for representation issues, intra-union and inter-union disputes, the Employees Compensation Commission for claims against the State Insurance Fund, and the Bureau of Employment Services, the Overseas Employment Development Board and the National Seamans Board which later were fused into the Philippine Overseas Employment Administration on matters involving overseas Filipino workers, both land-based and sea-based.

STRUCTURE OF THE NLRC

The NLRC is a two-tiered administrative or quasi-judicial body manned at the lower level by Labour Arbiters, and at the appellate level by the Commission proper. The National Labour Relations Commission, before its reconstitution, was tripartite in composition and consisted of the Minister of Labour as Chairman, and three (3) members each representing the public, the workers, and the employers. Under Executive Order No. 47 issued by the President on 10 September 1986, the NLRC was restructured in line with the government programme to professionalise the labour dispute settlement machinery. Sectoral representation was removed and the NLRC as presently constituted consists of the Minister of Labour and Employment as Chairman and nine (9) Commissioners. In the absence of the Minister of Labour, his duly authorized Deputy Minister acts as Chairman.

The Commissioners shall have at least five (5) years experience in handling labour-management relations while the Executive Labour Arbiters and Labour Arbiters must be members of the bar with at least two (2) years experience in the same field. The Commissioners receive an annual salary of not less than eighty-seven thousand (P87,000) pesos while the Labour Arbiters get not less than seventy-two thousand (P72,000) pesos. The Commissioners are appointed by the President for a term of six (6) years without prejudice to reappointment. Of the Commissioners first appointed, three shall hold office for six (6) years. The Executive Labour Arbiters and Labour Arbiters are also appointed by the President but subject to civil service law, rules and regulations.

The Commission sits *en banc* or in three divisions, each composed of three members. It determines, by rules approved by the Chairman, the cases it shall decide *en banc* and those to be decided by a division. The decision of a division has the force and effect of a decision of the Commission. The Minister of Labour exercises administrative supervision over the Commission, its regional branches and their personnel. The Presiding Commissioner of the First Division acts as the Vice-Chairman of the Commission and is its day-to-day administrator. Each regional branch headed by an Executive Labour Arbiter is staffed with as many Labour Arbiters as shall be necessary for its effective operation. There are one-hundred four (104) Labour Arbiters throughout the country.

Under the proposed ministry-wide reorganization, the NLRC will be retained as an attached agency with practically the same structure except that the name will be changed to National Labour Arbitration Commission and one of the nine (9) Commissioners will be appointed a full-time Chairman in lieu of the Minister of Labour. The Chairman will receive a salary which is one range higher than the current salary of Commissioners.

JURISDICTION

The Labour Arbiters have original and exclusive jurisdiction to hear and decide the following cases involving all workers, whether agricultural or non-agricultural:

– unfair labour practice cases;

– those that workers may file involving wages, hours of work, and other terms and conditions of employment;

– all money claims of workers, including those based on non-payment or under-payment of wages, overtime compensation, separation pay, and other benefits provided for by law or appropriate agreement, except claims for employees compensation, social security, medicare and maternity benefits;

– cases involving household services;

– cases arising from any violation of Article 265 of the Labour Code regarding prohibited activities during strikes/lockouts including questions involving the legality of strikes/lockouts.

– termination cases;

– claims for moral or similar forms of damages arising from employee-employer relationship; and

– cases involving violation of compromise agreements or where there is prima facie evidence that the settlement was obtained through fraud, misrepresentation or coercion.

The Commission *en banc* exercises original and exclusive jurisdiction over the following:

– injunction cases;

– cases of contempt committed against the Commission or any of its members; and

– cases certified to the Commission by the Minister of Labour and Employment.

The Commission has exclusive appellate jurisdiction over the following:

– all cases decided by Labour Arbiters;

– appealed cases assigned to any of the Divisions of such complicated nature or involving such intricate questions of law that, upon the vote of a majority, are referred to the Commission *en banc* for action or resolution;

– any appealed cases if in the judgment of the Chairman or the Vice-Chairman of the Commission the disposition of the same by the Commission *en banc* is imperative because of policy implications and other justifiable grounds;

– contempt cases on appeal.

Other appealed cases are divided and distributed more or less equally, by raffle, assignment or otherwise, as directed by the Vice-Chairman of the Commission, among the Divisions for resolution.

COMPULSORY ARBITRATION PROCEDURES

The NLRC promulgated on 5 November 1986 its Revised Rules governing arbitration proceedings before the Labour Arbiters and the Commission. The Rules are intended to be construed to carry out the objectives of the Constitution and the Labour Code of the Philippines, which is to assist the parties in obtaining just, expeditious and inexpensive settlement of labour disputes.

One of the distinctive features of the rules is the use of a "position paper" to shorten the proceedings and to "de-legalise or de-judicialise" the same. A position paper is a statement under oath of a party's position in a case, accompanied by proofs in support of such position, together with the nature of the testimony of witness or witnesses to be presented. Supporting proofs usually consist of affidavits and other documents that tend to substantiate the party's position.

After submission of position papers, the Labour Arbiter shall determine whether there is a necessity for further hearing or investigation. If he finds the documents presented sufficient as to enable him to decide the case intelligently, he will proceed to do so after notifying the parties of such course of action and the reasons therefor. If he needs additional facts, evidence or clarification of specific points, he may elicit the desired information by questioning the parties or their witnesses or by requiring the submission of additional documentary evidence.

The Labour Arbiter may also conduct further hearings with the active participation of the parties or their counsels, but he is supposed to take full control of the proceedings and shall see to it that it is not litigious and technical. A great majority of cases are decided by Labour Arbiters on the basis of the parties' position papers alone, usually with the agreement of the parties.

The Commission proper operates in much the same way as Labour Arbiters do with respect to original cases. Appealed cases are also decided without the usual formalities obtaining in proceedings before appellate courts. Approaches do vary from one Arbiter or Commissioner to another but the underlying principle of the non-litigious nature of the proceedings is observed more or less uniformly.

EFFECTIVENESS OF COMPULSORY ARBITRATION

The number of cases being brought to compulsory arbitration is steadily increasing. From 1980 to 1985, for example, the reported aggregate cases being filed before the NLRC and the regional arbitration branches each year are as follows: 8,546 for 1980, 10,917 for 1981, 17,913 for 1982, 16,761 for 1983, 15,087 for 1984, 13,656 for 1985.

In terms of disposition, the regional arbitration branches registered 76.3 per cent rate of disposition in 1980; 69 per cent in 1981; 69.9 per cent in 1982; 65.4 per cent in 1983; 60.5 per cent in 1984; and 42.5 per cent in 1985. The Commission proper, on the other hand, has a rate of disposition of 48.9 per cent in 1980, 64.7 per cent in 1981, 84.1 per cent in 1982, 76.1 per cent in 1983, 60.80 per cent in 1984 and 76.5 per cent in 1985. It usually takes an average of three months from filing for a case to be heard and decided by Labour Arbiters; while a longer period of six months on the average is needed for the Commission to dispose of the same. Under the rules, the Labour Arbiters and the NLRC have 30 days after submission to dispose of a case.

The percentage of cases decided by Labour Arbiters and elevated to the NLRC on appeal are as follows: 38 per cent in 1980, 25 per cent in 1981, 17.29 per cent in 1982, 25.3 per cent in 1983, 26.4 per cent in 1984, and 48.7 per cent in 1985. NLRC decisions brought on appeal to the Supreme Court by way of certiorari represent about 10-12 per cent of cases decided, 90 per cent of which are affirmations and only 10 per cent are denials.

The law and the rules do not prohibit the Arbiters and Commissioners from conciliating cases subject to arbitration. In fact, they are most effective if they are able to help the parties reach mutually acceptable agreements instead of deciding the case. From year to year, the cases that are settled through conciliation are estimated at about twenty per cent (20 per cent) of the total cases filed before the Commission and the Labour Arbiters. In 1985, cases settled amicably constitute 18.94 per cent of the total cases reported disposed and adjudicated.

The yearly backlog of cases pending before the Commission proper are as follows: 1,082 in 1981, 1,219 in 1982, 527 in 1983, 910 in 1984 and 1,074 in 1985. At the Arbitration Branches, the figures are: 2,360 in 1980, 2,492 in 1981, 4,228 in 1982, 5,949 in 1983, 6,741 in 1984, 7,288 in 1985. The total aggregates of backlog of cases are: 2,360 in 1980, 3,574 in 1981, 5,447 in 1982, 6,476 in 1983, 7,651 in 1984 and 8,362 in 1985.

EFFECT OF COMPULSORY ARBITRATION AND COLLECTIVE BARGAINING

Compulsory arbitration applies to both rights and interests disputes. It is a mechanism, insofar as rights disputes are concerned, made available by government to a large segment of the workforce who are unorganized and who have no effective means of enforcing their rights under the law. About seventy per cent (70 per cent) of cases handled by the arbitration arm involve claims of individual workers who are either victims of illegal dismissal or have not received wages, allowances and other benefits provided for by law. Compulsory arbitration is intended to give them adequate protection against unfair and exploitative practices that may be resorted to by employers. Most cases of this nature are settled amicably by the parties with the assistance of Labour Arbiters who are required by law and rules to set aside the initial hearing for the purpose of helping the parties find ways and means to arrive at an amicable settlement. Compulsory arbitration will only come into full play after the Arbiter is satisfied that there is no more possibility of settlement.

The question of compatibility between collective bargaining and compulsory arbitration applies more to interest disputes when impasse or deadlock in collective bargaining negotiations has occurred and workers are left with no alternative but to resort to strike to enforce their demands. Under the law and practice in the Philippines, strike as a weapon of last resort is available to the workers and their unions subject to compliance with certain procedural requirements. Compulsory arbitration may be resorted to only in exceptional cases where work stoppages caused by strikes adversely affect the national interest as determined and certified by the Minister of Labour and Employment.

For compulsory arbitration to be consistent and effective in these cases, the following conditions must be satisfied. First, it must be used only in strictly "national interest cases" or those involving essential services where the interruption of such activities would endanger the life, personal safety or health of the whole or part of the population. Any indiscriminate or premature use of the power to certify cases to compulsory arbitration will only serve to negate the law and policy objectives favouring collective bargaining in lieu of arbitration. Second, the arbitration system itself must be able to command the respect of the parties in the sense that the machinery is working efficiently and manned by people with known competence, impartiality and integrity. If it is to serve the national interest and that of the parties involved, excessive legalism and delays must be avoided and the award or decision must be seen by both parties as fair, just and equitable. Otherwise, the whole system is likely to collapse and collective bargaining will become meaningless.

IMPROVEMENTS IN THE SYSTEM

As already mentioned, the reforms already put into effect by the new government include the following:

- structural changes in the NLRC in line with the programme to professionalise the labour dispute settlement system;

- appointment of competent personnel taking into account not only their technical competence but also their integrity, and honesty and dedication to the service;

- upgrading of salaries of Commissioners and Labour Arbiters commensurate to their level of degree of responsibilities;

- promulgation of revised rules of proceedings to facilitate the speedy and fair disposition of cases, and

- re-orientation programmes and seminars for Labour Arbiters and other labour relations personnel on the new labour relations thrusts and the rules of proceedings governing arbitration.

It is expected that the structural reforms will be complemented by corresponding budgetary allocations necessary to make the entire machinery work with optimum efficiency. It is also hoped that corresponding reforms among labour and management practitioners will also be effected by their respective sectors to ensure tripartite efforts in achieving the goals of fair, economical and speedy labour justice.

LEGAL CONCEPTS AND PRINCIPLES

The law and policy on voluntary and compulsory arbitration as practiced in the Philippines have evolved some basic legal concepts and principles which could be of interest to other ASEAN countries depending on their particular situation. One is the concept of "economic" and "rights" disputes which is of American orientation and requires distinct delineation insofar as their mode of labour dispute resolution is concerned. Economic disputes would refer to unresolved issues in collective negotiations which are settled through free collective bargaining including the use of strikes and which may be the subject of compulsory arbitration only through certification by the Minister of Labour. Rights disputes, on the other hand, are by law the proper subjects of arbitration.

The other concept refers to the so-called "national interest cases" which in other ASEAN countries are more often referred to as disputes affecting "essential services". The nature of these cases and whether they may be certified to compulsory arbitration or not, are subject to the determination of the Labour Minister and may be questioned only before the highest court of the land, the Supreme Court. In these cases, compulsory arbitration is viewed and treated as a better alternative to prolonged strikes. The effectiveness of the approach depends on the speed in resolving the cases and the acceptability of the award or decision to both parties.

Another distinct feature of the arbitration system is its "de-judicialised" nature characterized by decisions based on "position papers" instead of full-blown judicial hearings that require longer resolution times. Other innovative approaches to achieve speedy and economical labour justice continue to be of interest to government and it is hoped that, in due time, the labour arbitration system in the country will truly be reflective of the aspirations of the workers and employers and the government as a whole.

VOLUNTARY AND COMPULSORY ARBITRATION OF LABOUR DISPUTES IN SINGAPORE

by

Mr. Tan Boon Chiang,
President, Industrial Arbitration Court, Singapore

INTRODUCTION

In Singapore, the industrial arbitration process provided by the Industrial Relations Act in Parts IV (arbitration), V (awards) and VI (procedures and powers of the Industrial Arbitration Court) covers entirely all salient aspects of voluntary and compulsory arbitration. The provisions are tailored to the needs of the country. They allow the optional referral of disputes to voluntary arbitration and, at the same time where the public interest demands it, empower the Minister for Labour to refer compulsorily such disputes to arbitration.

VOLUNTARY ARBITRATION

Section 31 of Part IV of the Industrial Relations Act provides that where:

– all the trade unions and employers who are parties to a trade dispute jointly make a request in writing to the Registrar that the trade dispute be submitted to arbitration; or

– a trade union or an employer who is a party to a trade dispute makes a request in writing to the Registrar that pursuant to subsection (6) of section 48 or subsection (3) of section 49 of the Employment Act the trade dispute be submitted to arbitration;

The Court shall have cognizance of the trade dispute. These two provisions enable:

– voluntary arbitration to be put into motion by either a joint application by trade unions and employers referring disputes to the Court; or

– either a trade union or an employer under the provisions of section 48(6) and section 49(3) of the Employment Act to refer trade disputes to arbitration.

In a sense it is only in the first instance, where both the trade union and employer as parties to a dispute make a joint request to the Registrar, that voluntary arbitration would arise. In the case of either party applying under section 48(6) or 49(3) of the Employment Act, the process, once initiated by the party who has decided to refer the dispute to arbitration under the enabling powers, will compel the other party to submit their dispute to arbitration.

On the filing of the application to the Industrial Arbitration Court, subject to the provisions of section 33 of the Industrial Relations Act which deals with disputes as to employment in Government service, and subject also to certain limitations laid down for reference to the President of Singapore, the Court will normally proceed to hear such applications to determine the dispute.

PROVISION FOR SETTING UP THE INDUSTRIAL ARBITRATION COURT

The application of these referral provisions puts into motion the arbitration process. The Court can thereupon be constituted and proceed to determine the dispute as efficiently and rapidly as possible. The jurisdiction of the Court is unlimited. Representation before it may comprise the accredited officer of the union representing the employees of the particular firm concerned and the employer respectively. The Government as an employer is represented by an officer of the Ministry of Finance if a dispute involving the Government is being determined. Where the dispute, and the cognizance in regard to the trade dispute, is in relation to employment in Government service, the President of the Industrial Arbitration Court shall so inform the President of Singapore and the Court shall not exercise its powers or perform its functions in relation to the trade dispute, so far as it relates to that employment, except with the approval of the President of Singapore. Apart from this, in all other respects, the arbitration process applicable to the private sector applies equally to the public sector. Awards made by the Court are binding upon government in the same manner as those which are binding upon private enterprises. In determining a dispute the Court shall, in accordance with section 34 of the Industrial Relations Act, have regard:

– not only to the interests of the persons immediately concerned but to the interests of the community as a whole and in particular to the condition of the economy of Singapore; and

– the recommendations made from time to time by the Minister under section 51 of the Employment Act relating to matters specified in that section.

Except where otherwise provided in the Industrial Relations Act, the Court shall, in relation to any trade dispute of which it has cognizance, or any other matter with regard to which it has jurisdiction under the Act, be constituted by the President or the Deputy President and two members selected from the employer and employee panels constituted under the Act. The President has the same rights, privileges, protection and immunity as a judge of the Supreme Court.

The provisions of the Constitution relating to the tenure of office and the terms of office of judges of the Supreme Court shall be deemed to apply to him as if he were a judge of the Supreme Court. The Deputy President shall in the performance of his functions and duties have the same protection and immunity as the President.

The two panels of the Court, one for the employer and the other for the employee, consist of ten members each appointed by the Minister through notification in the Government Gazette. To do this the Minister may from time to time invite –

– a trade union of employers to nominate seven suitable persons for appointment to the employer panel, and the Minister of Finance to nominate three such persons, and

– a trade union of employees to similarly nominate ten suitable persons for appointment to the employee panel.

A person is deemed to be a suitable person for appointment to a panel if he is eligible in accordance with Section 7 of the Industrial Relations Act and is in the opinion of the Minister of Labour a fit and proper person to be selected to be a member of the Court. He must not be an undischarged bankrupt or of unsound mind, or a non-citizen of Singapore or a person who has been convicted of contempt of Court, or has within the previous three years been convicted of an offence under the Trade Disputes Act or the Industrial Relations Act. A person who is an employee shall not be eligible to be a member of the employer panel and vice versa an employer shall not be eligible to serve on the employee panel. The appointment of a panel member shall be for an initial period of one year but he is eligible for reappointment. The Minister has powers to remove a panel member from any panel subject to certain conditions laid down in Section 9 of the Industrial Relations Act.

For the purpose of constituting a Court for the determination of a trade dispute or any other industrial matter, the President determines who are the disputing parties and invites the trade union and the employer to each select a member of the employee and employer panels respectively. Following selection, the President declares that members selected constitute together with him the Court for the purposes of the trade dispute. If a member is not selected, the President will notify the Minister for Labour who will make the selection and the member thus selected will be declared a member of the Court by the President. Should a member after the constitution of the Court become unable to hear or to continue to hear or determine the trade dispute or industrial matter, or through death or for other reason the member ceases to be a Panel Member, the Court will have to be reconstituted as provided for in order to continue the hearing taking regard of the evidence given, the arguments adduced and any interim award made during the previous hearing. A member of the Court shall, in the performance of his functions and duties under the Act, have the same protection and immunity as the President. Panel members are required to take an oath of allegiance and the judicial oath.

Registrars and other assigned officers of the Court, apart from their administrative duties, have been utilised to provide informal conciliation though this is not specifically a statutory function. Their efforts in this direction have been specially authorised by order of the Court and their rate of success in conciliatory efforts, at the doorstep of the Court, has indicated clearly that this is a function and service which the Court should without doubt continue to offer to disputing parties. Very often, as a last resort, such conciliation and the skills developed by the registrars and other officers of the Court over the years have been instrumental in persuading the parties to settle their dispute amicably out of Court without the attendant publicity and other embarrassing consequences of litigation in open Court.

VOLUNTARY REFERENCE OF DISPUTES TO ARBITRATION

It must be borne in mind that the arbitration process is part of the machinery of industrial relations which has been evolved through practice, and refined and processed by legislation. Over the years, the machinery has been kept relevant and amendments made where necessary to bring it up-to-date with the needs of the country at different stages of its development. The machinery is designed to provide at every stage of the relationship between employers and employees, a remedy for any differences that may arise without the need for the parties to resort to extreme industrial action. Because human relationships are so complex, no system is entirely fool-proof or perfect. Hence from time to time the machinery of industrial relations in Singapore, though admirable in many respects, has not been able to cover every situation. Nevertheless, by and large, the relevancy of the machinery has been maintained.

Arbitration forms the tail-end of the system. It is normally resorted to as a remedy of last resort when the relationship between employer and employee suffers a setback or reaches an impasse and a dispute arises. Many disputes and industrial matters are in fact settled at lower levels and do not go beyond the factory floor or the company or the enterprise level. However, the more cogent issues may be referred to the Ministry of Labour for assistance in resolution and the more fundamental, basic and complex gut issues may eventually be referred to arbitration.

Voluntary arbitration has been practised and accepted freely in Singapore. The parties have over the years indicated willingness to refer of their own accord their seemingly insoluable disputes for determination by the Industrial Arbitration Court. Although there was initial apprehension as to the general acceptability of voluntary arbitration, this initial hesitation has long since disappeared.

Over the years, the Court has established a reputation for impartiality in full pursuance of its statutory mandate to determine disputes in equity, good conscience and the substantial merits of the case without regard to technicalities and legal forms.

Confidence in the Court has grown and the parties, now more mature and aware of the Court's record, have willingly brought their disputes voluntarily to arbitration. Voluntary reference is therefore widely practised. Industrial parties willingly continue of their own volition to refer disputes to the Industrial Arbitration Court for determination. Although in the initial stages of their disputes, parties realise that they are the best arbitrators of their own differences, as soon as they reach an impasse, even after reference to their own personnel or following assistance from the Ministry of Labour, they willingly submit their disputes to arbitration.

In disputes over interest, the Court is normally constituted as provided under the Industrial Relations Act. In certain disputes over rights and in legal interpretation, however, the President has powers to sit alone to determine the dispute (section 59). Hearings of the Court proceed in accordance with procedures determined by the Court subject to the provisions of the Act and regulations made thereunder. The Act provides that the Court shall not be bound in a formal manner but has powers to inform itself of any matter in such a manner as it thinks just, always acting according to equity, good conscience and the substantial merits of the case. Technicalities, legal forms and procedures are thus kept to a minimum without loss of decorum or formality in the process. Decisions made by the Court can either be unanimous, or by a majority, or where the views of the three members of the Court differ entirely from each other, the decision of the President shall prevail. No stalemate is therefore possible and a finality in the award of the Court can be reached. The Court's jurisdiction is unlimited and in all court matters the Court has the status of a high court. Its awards are final and conclusive and are not subject to any challenge, appeal, review. They cannot be quashed or be called in question in any court nor be subject to any prerogative writs on any account except of course to the principles of natural justice.

EFFECTIVENESS OF THE ARBITRATION PROCESS – ITS STRENGTHS AND WEAKNESSES

Over the 26 years that the Court has been in existence, its decisions have been effective in settling basic and crucial issues and in erasing doubts over the interpretation of many provisions of the Act and terms of collective agreements. Basic decisions on the extent of fringe benefits and terms and conditions of employment have also been embodied in the awards and laid down as precedence over the years. The encouragement which has always been given to the parties to maintain strong rapport in their relationship with one another, and the willingness of industrial parties to accord full support to this attitude, has resulted in a more healthy and peaceful industrial relations climate. Such extreme industrial action as strikes have been almost non-existent over the last eight years. Only a minimum of disputes have been referred to arbitration. Parties are more willing to find their own solutions without reference to the Ministry of Labour or to the Court. This rapport continues to date. Many industrial parties consider that litigation in Court would be tantamount to an admission of a breakdown in good industrial relations and hence seek solutions themselves. They are encouraged by their respective organisations, the government and the Court. Such attitudes show maturity and augur well for industrial relations in Singapore.

Arbitration and the whole machinery of industrial relations remains available as always but has been particularly beneficial during the recent economic recession. Parties have been even more subdued in their confrontation with one another, if ever there was any, and have more readily reached amicable solutions over differences in their relationship and in determination of terms and conditions of employment. The situation will not always remain the same. Sacrifices which workers and employers have been asked to make during the current period of economic recession could lead to a more open attitude for better working terms and conditions as Singapore pulls out of recession and moves into more vital economic activity. As always, the arbitration process will continue to exercise its effective edge.

In the immediate preceding paragraphs the strength of the arbitration system has been set out in some detail. Industrial parties know that fairness, impartiality, and the determination of disputes in equity and in good conscience according to the substantial merits of their respective cases has established the Court as a vital link in the industrial relations machinery. The co-operation, respect and willingness to refer disputes to the Court are additional testimony to the effectiveness of the system. However, it was never the intention to establish a Court to provide a panacea for all industrial ills It may not be possible to provide perfect final solutions to problems which even the disputing parties themselves have done their utmost to solve.

One of the bottle-necks which has arisen in the arbitration process is the panel system itself. Parties have tended to exercise definite choices and preferences for certain panel members and not others. As a result, the workload of panel members has not been evenly distributed, causing difficulty in the speedy resolution of disputes as certain members are over-taxed while others are available but not selected. The complexity of certain disputes has also prolonged the arbitration process. Awards have been at times not as speedily available as they should be. The appointment of panel members, currently for a term of one year subject to re-appointment, has assisted in providing a more rapid turnover of talent and the possibility of changes in panel membership if that is required.

What is more important is that voluntary arbitration has always been developed and upheld as a machinery of last resort. Consequently disputing parties, as they enter the last stages before commencement of litigation, very often become more amenable to possible solutions which had previously been rejected. The Court has found that even slight encouragement to disputing parties to try once more to find a solution themselves, frequently with the assistance of the Registrar of the Court, as encouraged or directed by the Court, has helped them reach a settlement at the very doorstep of the Court. Where understanding and reasonably good relationships exist, the willingness to resolve a dispute among themselves assumes a powerful priority.

The process of keeping the Court and its procedures up to date and relevant at all times in order to maintain its effectiveness is a continuing one. Industrial relations is a living relationship which develops with time and circumstances. Where change is necessary, change will be made, as has been done in the past. Where amendments to legal provisions are clearly needed such changes have been made to the enabling statutes. The machinery of industrial relations must and will always be kept up-to-date and relevant to meet the challenges of the times, however trying the economic and other conditions.

COMPULSORY ARBITRATION

Section 31 of the Industrial Relations Act provides that the Court shall have cognizance of a trade dispute where –

– the Minister by notice in the Gazette directs that the trade dispute be submitted to arbitration; or

– the President of Singapore by proclamation declares that by reason of special circumstances it is essential in the public interest that a trade dispute be submitted to arbitration.

In such cases the parties have no choice. They are compelled to bring their dispute to the Court for determination however unwilling they may be. The appointment of panel members, the tripartite composition of the Court, the procedures and discretion of the Court subject to statutory provisions, and the hearing and determination of disputes are, of course, identical to voluntary arbitration and need not be repeated here.

Initially, when the Act was passed in 1960 and the Industrial Arbitration Court was set up, there was a fear that compulsory arbitration might bring undesirable consequences by forcing unwilling parties to submit their dispute to arbitration. Unions were perhaps fearful that the better resources available to employers would enable them to present and adduce evidence before the Court in a more effective way so as to establish their supremacy in any dispute. Employers, on the other hand, were also concerned that compulsory powers could be unreasonably exercised and disputes over sensitive issues, which in their view ought not to be openly argued before the Court, could be dragged into the open with its undue and attendant publicity. Over the years, these views have receded considerably. Successive data published in the Annual Reports of the President of the Industrial Arbitration Court have clearly established that the compulsory aspect of arbitration and the fears that initially surrounded it are now unimportant and unfounded. The following table, drawn from the Annual Report for 1986 shows clearly the minimal compulsory references made over the years. It clearly indicates that in the last six years not a single dispute was referred compulsorily to the Court.

COMPARATIVE TABLE OF VOLUNTARY AND COMPULSORY REFERENCES TO THE COURT 1960-1986

Year	*Total No. of Cases*	*Voluntary Applications Sections 16 (4), 31 (a), 31 (b), 38 (4), 42 (5), 43, 44, 45, 55 and 56*	*Compulsory References By Direction. Sections 31 (c) and 31 (d)*
1960/61	25	16 (64.0%)	9 (36.0%)
1962	45	37 (82.2%)	8 (17.8%)
1963	132	121 (91.6%)	11 (8.4%)
1964	210	197 (93.7%)	13 (6.3%)
1965	88	77 (87.5%)	11 (12.5%)
1966	100	99 (99.0%)	1 (1.0%)
1967	78	75 (96.2%)	3 (3.8%)
1968	46	46 (100.0%)	–
1969	48	48 (100.0%)	–
1970	47	43 (91.5%)	4 (8.5%)
1971	44	43 (97.6%)	1 (2.4%)
1972	81	79 (97.5%)	2 (2.5%)
1973	207	206 (99.5%)	1 (0.5%)
1974	142	141 (99.3%)	1 (0.7%)
1975	137	133 (97.1%)	4 (2.9%)
1976	161	158 (98.1%)	3 (1.9%)
1977	116	113 (97.4%)	3 (2.6%)
1978	116	115 (99.1%)	1 (0.9%)
1979	156	155 (99.4%)	1 (0.6%)
1980	194	191 (98.5%)	3 (1.5%)
1981	148	148 (100.0%)	–
1982	116	116 (100.0%)	–
1983	106	106 (100.0%)	–
1984	73	73 (100.0%)	–
1985	72	72 (100.0%)	–
1986	111	111 (100.0%)	–

EFFECTIVENESS OF COMPULSORY ARBITRATION

Disputes involving the government as a party are equally subject to the procedures laid down by the Court and the government is bound by its awards in the same manner as private industrial parties. The awards have thus effectively determined disputes which in the public interest needed to be resolved. The Court has thus in the past determined the terms and conditions of employment of nurses in government hospitals, immigration and custom officers, clerical officers and other categories of government employees. To this day, successive collective agreements follow awards of the Court covering certain categories of government officers. Such agreements implement and extend Court awards to counter obsolescence and to bring up-to-date terms and conditions of service prevailing in the public sector. Because of the relatively rare occurrence of compulsory reference of such disputes their numbers may appear insignificient. However, their effectiveness goes beyond the awards themselves in the sense that the consequences of the award are reflected over a wider sphere of employment relationship than the mere parties themselves. For the Court has always been required to have regard not only to the interest of the parties immediatley concerned but to the interests of the community as a whole and in particular the economic condition of Singapore. It must also take into consideration the recommendations made from time to time by the Minister under section 51 of the Employment Act: that is to say, to take into regard the Minister's powers, exercised by notification in the Gazette, to suspend the application of any of the provisions of the relevant part of the Employment Act to any class of employees when the public interest so requires it.

The parties to compulsory awards have generally willingly accepted them. They have by and large been glad to have their difficult issues resolved by the Court. As the awards are final and conclusive, such acceptance carries added meaning. The length or period of awards is the same for both voluntary and compulsory cases. It may stretch to a maximum of three years and a minimum of two years. The awards are taken as criteria for future negotiations with a view to settling a new or fresh collective agreement, as the case may be. Parties have found that these awards act very much as guidelines for the determination of provisions in future collective agreements. The effectiveness of the machinery for compulsory arbitration is thus indicated by its far-reaching consequences.

COMPULSORY ARBITRATION AND COLLECTIVE BARGAINING

One of the favourite controversies among arbitration practitioners has always been whether compulsory arbitration would either impair or promote collective bargaining. A large body of opinion holds the first view. One school of thought even suggests that compulsory arbitration and collective bargaining are mutually exclusive. For if industrial parties accept the machinery for collective bargaining, they must be allowed of their own accord through such bargaining to find solutions or acceptable terms and conditions of employment without let or hindrance. They hold the view that 'let or hindrance' may occur if the parties are under constant threat that the enabling executive may refer or direct their differences to compulsory arbitration. This would pre-empt any possibility of a solution through collective bargaining. What is worse, such powers to direct parties and their differences to compulsory arbitration might be exercised before all voluntary attempts at a solution are exhausted.

The view that prevails in Singapore on the other hand subscribes to the view that compulsory arbitration is mutually complementary with collective bargaining. The system Singapore has chosen for itself provides for a reasonable dispute settlement machinery at every level of relationship so that no vacuum should in fact exist. Where differences arise at any level, there should be available a portion of that machinery to settle those differences. Thus if parties are encouraged to collectively bargain, they could use the machinery to do so and attempt their level best to reach a solution. It is only when all means of solution have been exhausted through collective bargaining and the parties themselves are still unable to reach consensus that they should refer their dispute to arbitration. The authorities and the Minister with enabling powers will not interfere or exercise their discretion to either voluntary or compulsory arbitration unless it is clear that the parties have exhausted all means to resolve their dispute and have been unable to do so. Thus, in Singapore collective bargaining can exist, and has existed all these years, side by side with voluntary and compulsory arbitration. There has never been at any time any difficulty or irritation which might have impaired collective bargaining which has arisen from the joint presence of both approaches in a single system. Compulsory arbitration has always and will always continue to complement collective bargaining. Over the years, industrial parties, that is, trade unions, employers and employees have been fully aware that if they have available both machineries side by side, the possibility of reaching a solution over their differences can and will be found at the appropriate level. Relationships can be maintained and there need never be any recourse to industrial action of any kind, minor or extreme.

RELEVANCE OF COMPULSORY ARBITRATION

As the system of compulsory arbitration exists at the moment there is no need for any change or improvement. Its use by ministerial executive action has been very sparing and responsibly exercised. Industrial parties whether employers or employees have not felt any undue pressure or disadvantage affecting their relationship at any time through such exercise. Initial fears of compulsory arbitration and its dire consequences have been dispelled. Today in Singapore parties accept that the powers of compulsorily directing a dispute to arbitration can and will be exercised responsibly and not with undue pressure; and that such a power adds body and roundness to the machinery of industrial relations to enhance the constant quest for industrial peace with justice for the establishment of economic well-being for the country.

The acceptance of the Singaporean system in other ASEAN countries will depend upon the assessments these countries make of their own situation and the applicability of the Singapore system in the context of their own. Just as Singapore has found a system which was applicable elsewhere, but which it tailored to meet its own needs, so must ASEAN countries do likewise. They may tailor Singapore's system if they wish to meet their own particular economic needs. The concept and legal principles laid down for the operation of the court, particularly impartiality and informality, equity and good conscience, could be a few of the aspects which could be generally applicable; but again the choice must rest with the ASEAN countries concerned. They themselves would be able to determine what is best for their needs.

VOLUNTARY AND COMPULSORY ARBITRATION OF LABOUR DISPUTES IN THAILAND

by

Mr. Pisit Jongstavoravong,
Office of the Arbitrators, Ministry of Interior, Thailand.

INTRODUCTION

Labour disputes, a natural characteristic of any industrial relations system, include the whole range of differences of opinion and objectives that can cause feelings of discord between individuals or groups of people in industry; i.e. the employers and employees. In whatever way a dispute is manifested, it is sure to cause inconvenience, loss of production and increased cost, especially when the parties decide to strike or lock-out. The methods and machineries for the settlement of labour disputes are therefore, a vital and integral part of a labour relations system. Considering the various labour dispute settlement machineries, collective bargaining will be the first stage. But whenever continued collective bargaining appears to the parties to be futile, then conciliation or mediation, the next stage, will be the way in which third parties can be brought in to help resolve the dispute and pave the way to voluntary agreement. The last stage is arbitration, a decision-making process, in which the parties to a dispute rely upon a third party to make a final judgement or award. Whether arbitration is voluntary or compulsory depends on the kind of dispute; i.e. whether rights or interest, involving public employees or not. For this reason the last stage, arbitration, could be considered as a substitute for work stoppages (strikes or lock-out).

In Thailand, according to the Labour Relations Act, B.E. 2518 (1975), when any group of employees, or labour union, or employer submits a claim or demand relating to conditions of employment to the other party, if there is no negotiation within three days or there is no agreement after negotiations for whatever reason, then a labour dispute shall be regarded as having occurred. The party which presented the demand shall notify the conciliation officer accordingly in writing within twenty-four hours. After this, the conciliation officer shall proceed to effect settlement of the dispute within five days of notification. If a settlement cannot be reached, there are two ways that remain for the parties to choose; the first one is to strike or lock-out, the other is voluntary arbitration.

In Thailand, voluntary arbitration is based on two principles: the first is that the parties are free to refer their case to arbitration voluntarily, the second is that the parties are free to select an arbitrator or a group of arbitrators. The purpose of providing this machinery is to reduce the damages caused by work stoppages (strike or lock-out) and also to promote industrial peace.

However, labour disputes in vital industries cannot use voluntary arbitration or resort to strike or lock-out. If there is a labour dispute in any vital industry, the conciliation officer shall refer the case to the Labour Relations Committee for compulsory arbitration.

VOLUNTARY ARBITRATION

"When there is a labour dispute. . . . . . ., the employer and employees, the parties concerned in the dispute, may appoint an arbitrator. . . . . . . "

This statement is the first provision of law on voluntary arbitration as a means of dispute settlement. It appeared in sections 117 and 118 of the Labour Act, B.E. 2499 (1956), the first labour law in Thailand. But at that time, disputants could appoint a voluntary arbitrator only with permission from the Labour Relations Committee. Hearing procedures, making the award and qualifications of arbitrators were as prescribed in the Civil Procedure Code B.E. 2477 (1934). There was no provision about any of these matters in the Labour Act.

After this Act was repealed in 1958, provisions on voluntary arbitration appeared in each subsequent law, but there were still no provisions about the proceedings and qualification of arbitrators. Then in 1966, the Ministry of Interior promulgated a Ministrial Regulation which determined arbitrators' qualifications, the regulations relating to their appointment and procedures for hearing and making the award. The Ministry also appointed the arbitrators' first secretary.

In 1972, by virtue of the Announcement of The National Executive Council No. 103, the Ministry of Interior promulgated a Notification Re : Labour Relations. This upheld the earlier regulations and also added provisions about the kinds of undertaking which shall refer their disputes to voluntary arbitration and penalties for not doing so.

At present, the laws relating to voluntary arbitration are to be found in the Labour Relations Act, B.E. 2518 (1975) and Ministrial Regulation No. 2 B.E. 2519 (1976) whose provisions on voluntary arbitration are as follows:

– Section 9 : establishment of the Office of the Arbitrator;

– Sections 22-23 and Ministrial Regulation No. 2 B.E. 2519 (1976): the kinds of labour dispute that may be referred to voluntary arbitration;

– Section 26 : how to refer a case to voluntary arbitration;

– Sections 27-30 : arbitration proceedings;

– Sections 31-32 and sections 134-135 : penalty provisions.

Figure 1. Labour Dispute Settlement Procedure

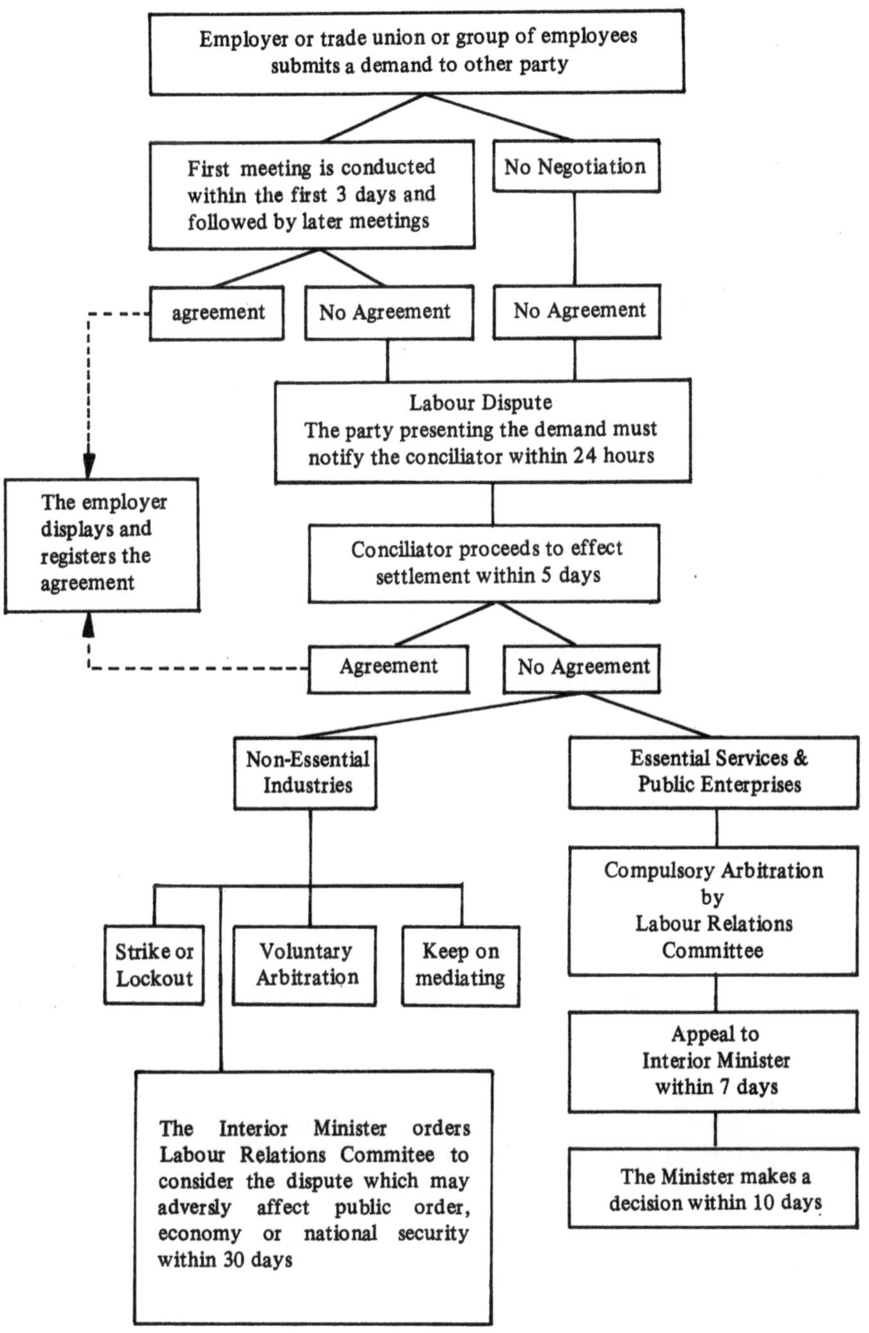

LAWS AND REGULATIONS

The entire spectrum of laws on voluntary arbitration can be found in the Civil and Commercial Code, the Civil Procedure Code and the Labour Relations Act B.E. 2518 (1975). Each law deals with different target groups and aspects. The Civil and Commercial Code and Civil Procedure Code cover all types of dispute but the Labour Relations Act deals specificially with labour disputes. These two main types of law are elaborated below.

Civil and Commercial Code and Civil Procedure Code

According to Sections 850-852 of Civil and Commercial Code and Sections 138-142 and 210-222 of the Civil Procedure Code, the law provides arbitration machinery for any type of dispute as follows:

Appointment : The parties can appoint arbitrator(s) in two ways:

– In the court : the parties may ask a judge to appoint arbitrators for the case after it has been submitted to the court but before a verdict is given;

– Out of the court : the parties may appoint arbitrator(s) before submitting the case to the court.

Number of arbitrators : When the parties agree to appoint an arbitrator, they can appoint in writing an arbitrator or a group of arbitrators. But if appointed by the court, only one arbitrator from each side is allowed.

Hearing and Award : In making the award, if there are many arbitrators, the award shall be by majority vote.

However, these provisions deal with general disputes enforceable by the Civil Court. The law that especially deals with labour disputes is the Labour Relations Act, 1975.

Labour Relations Act., B.E. 2518 (1975)

Coverage : According to Sections 22 and 23 of this Act and the Ministerial Regulation No. 2 B.E. 2519 (1976), if a labour dispute cannot be settled within five days from the date the conciliation officer is notified, it shall be regarded as one which cannot be settled. The parties (employer and employees) may agree to appoint an arbitrator and except in the following undertakings, the employer may effect a lock-out or the employees go on strike:

– Railway;

– Port;

– Telephone or telecommunication;

- Production or distribution of energy or electricity for the public;
- Water works;
- Production or refinery of oil fuel;
- Hospital or clinic;
- All undertakings by State enterprises pursuant to the law on budgetary appropriations;
- Private colleges and schools pursuant to the law on private colleges and the law on private schools;
- Undertakings by co-operatives under the law on co-operative societies;
- Land, water and air transport as well as supplementary undertakings of transport or in connection with transport at depot, harbour and airport and tourism;
- Sale of fuel oil pursuant to the law on fuel oil.

In addition, this act shall not apply to

- Central Administration;
- Provincial Administration;
- Local Administration;
- Bangkok Metropolitan Administration.

Authority to appoint an arbitrator and types of dispute covered : The persons who may agree to appoint an arbitrator(s) are an employer or group of employers, and employees or the trade union concerned in a dispute involving conditions of employment, or agreements relating to conditions of employment, or over employee rights under the Labour Relations Act, 1975 and Labour Protection Law, 1972.

Proceedings : As provided in Sections 26-30 of the Labour Relations Act, when there is a dispute which cannot be settled, the employer and employees may agree to appoint one or several arbitrators to decide it. Within seven days of the appointment, the arbitrator shall notify both parties of the date for submission of relevant information, and the date, time and place of the sitting of arbitrator(s).

During the arbitration proceedings, the arbitrator shall allow both parties to submit argument and produce witnesses. At the end of the proceedings, an award shall be made in writing which must contain at least the following particulars:

- date of the award;

- issues under dispute;
- facts as found in arbitration;
- reasons for the award;
- requirements to be carried out or refrained from by either or both parties.

The award shall be reached by majority vote and signed by the arbitrators.

Within three days from the date of the award, the arbitrator(s) shall deliver copies of it to both parties or to their representatives, and shall post another copy at the place where employees involved in the demand work. After this, the award shall be registered with the Director-General of Department of Labour, Ministry of Interior, or person entrusted by him, within fifteen days of the award. The award shall be effective for one year. A summary of these procedures is shown in Figure 2.

Penalty Provisions : In order to ensure that the arbitration procedures will operate conveniently, speedily, equitably and justly, and to prevent and protect both parties from unfair practices such as termination of employment, strike or lock-out, the Labour Relations Act also provides penalty provisions as follows:

"Section 31. When the demand has been notified under Section 13, if such demand is in the course of negotiation, settlement or arbitration on labour dispute under Section 13 to Section 29, the employer shall not dismiss or transfer from duty the employees, representatives of employees, Committee members or Sub-committee members of labour union or Committee members or Sub-committee members of labour federation involved in the demand, unless such persons:

(1) perform their duties dishonestly or intentionally commit a criminal offence against the employer;

(2) intentionally cause damage to the employer;

(3) violate the rules, regulations or lawful orders of the employer after written warning or caution has been given by the employer, except in a serious case the employer is not required to give warning or caution; provided, such rules, regulations or orders have not been issued for the purpose of preventing the said persons from carrying out the demands;

(4) neglect their duties for three consecutive days without justifiable reason.

"The employees, representatives of employees, Committee members, Sub-committee members or members of labour union or Committee members or Sub-committee members of labour federation involved in the demand shall not encourage or cause the strike.

Figure 2. Voluntary arbitration proceedings

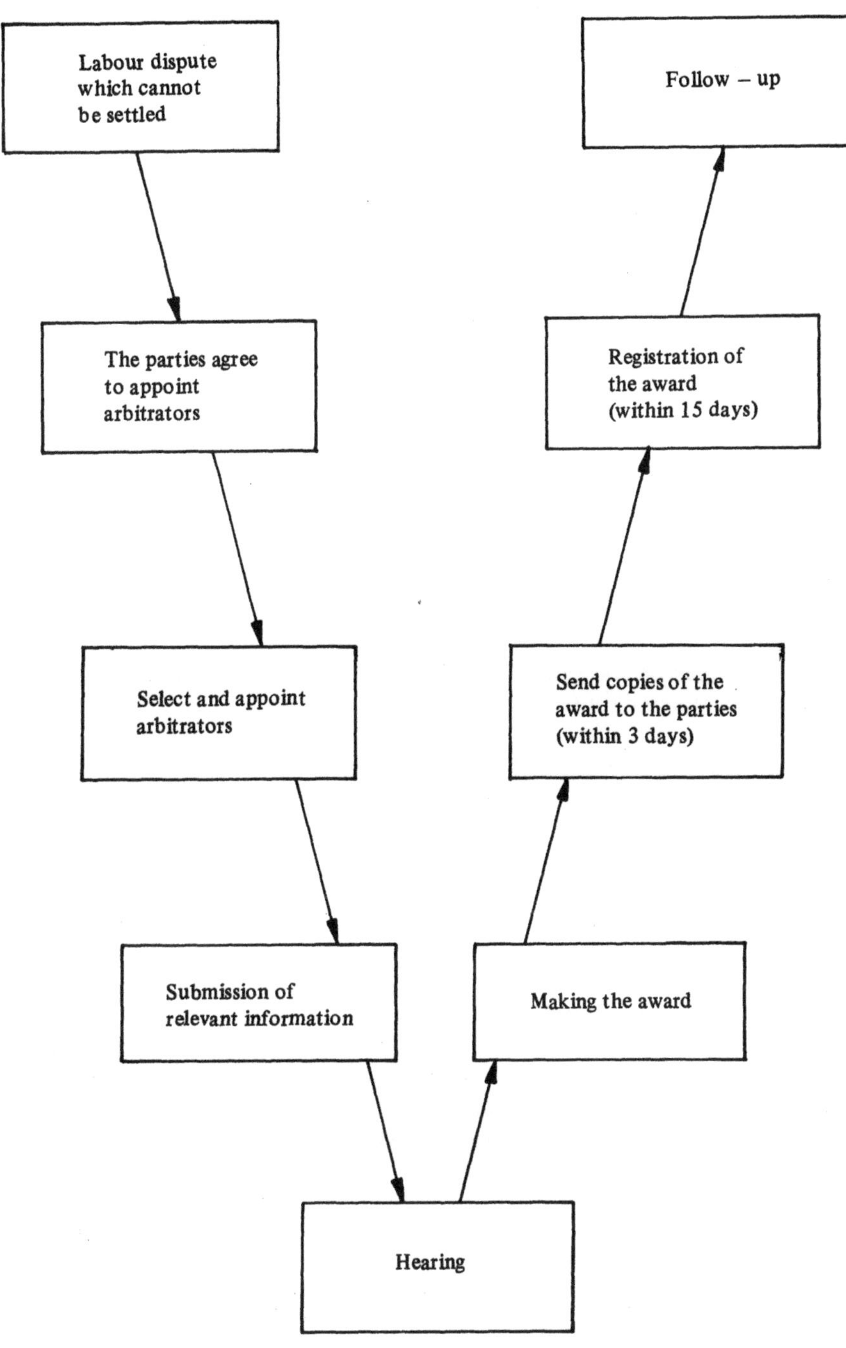

"Section 32. Persons not being employers, employees, Committee members of employers' association, labour union, employers' federation, labour federation, representatives or advisors involved in the demand shall not participate or join in any act relating to the demand, negotiation, settlement, arbitration on labour dispute, lock-out or strike gathering."

"Section 134. Any labour disputes arbitrator who accepts or agrees to accept money or properties from any person as inducement to decide a labour dispute so as to cause the employer, employee, employers' association or labour union to lose entitled benefit shall be liable to imprisonment for a term not exceeding one year or to a fine not exceeding twenty thousand Baht, or to both.

"Section 135. Any labour disputes arbitrator who fails to comply with Section 29 paragraph three or paragraph four shall be liable to a fine not exceeding one thousand Baht."

Organization : By virtue of section 9 of the Labour Relations Act, 1975, the Office of the Arbitrator was established in the Ministry of Interior in 1973. It has the following powers and duties:

– compile a list of names and qualifications of labour disputes arbitrators to be submitted to the parties for selection;

– supervise and carry out technical and administrative affairs relating to arbitration of labour disputes.

At present, the Office of the Arbitrator is attached to the Ministry of Interior, but is considered as part of the Labour Relations Division, Department of Labour, in terms of staff and budget. This office has three main functions:

– Administrative work : responsible for providing services to the arbitrator, arranges the place and facilities for arbitration sittings, sends copies of the award, and other general administrative work;

– Listing of arbitrators : compiles a list of names of arbitrators both in Bangkok Metropolis and the provinces; also classifies the arbitrators by professional capacity such as government officer, judge, business executive, representative of employers' confederation or trade union, university professor, politician or public personality. The present list contains over 200 names.

– Technical services and planning: provides data and information on economic and social affairs and other relevant topics to arbitrators, monitors the impact of voluntary arbitration, produces long and short-term plans to improve arbitration proceedings and promote voluntary arbitration. Publishes reports and documents on voluntary arbitration.

Arbitrator Qualifications: In compiling the list of arbitrators, the Office of the Arbitrator will consider only persons with certain qualifications:

- Having a good knowledge of both labour protection and labour relations, especially collective bargaining, and grievance procedures, and also with wide experience in interpreting collective bargaining agreements or those relating to conditions of employment, etc;
- of good moral character;
- acceptable to the parties.

Procedure to appoint arbitrators : In practice, when the parties refer a dispute to voluntary arbitration, the Office of the Arbitrator will offer them the list of arbitrators. The parties generally select a tripartite board of arbitrators, one each from the employer and employee sides and a third independent arbitrator. The Office may then invite the selected persons to arbitrate the case; if everyone accepts, the arbitration proceedings can begin. If any person declines, the parties must select another person and the officer may invite him. It only takes a short time to select and appoint the arbitrators.

AWARDS MADE BY VOLUNTARY ARBITRATION.

In fact, voluntary arbitration is not very popular. Athough the Labour Relations Act was promulgated in 1975, the Government in 1976 had to proclaim martial law. The Ministry of Interior therefore promulgated a Ministrial Regulation which prohibited employers and employees from strike or lock-out and which required all labour disputes to be referred to the Labour Relations Committe for compulsory arbitration.

In 1981, this Regulation was repealed. However, only 10 labour disputes have been referred to voluntary arbitration since then, two cases in the Bangkok Metropolitan area and eight cases in the provinces. Most cases were in the textile industry and none in commercial undertakings. Table 1 shows details of the cases.

Table 1. Number of cases referred to voluntary arbitration 1981-1986

Undertaking	*Regional Areas*	*Bangkok Metropolis*	*Total*
Textile	3	–	3
Metal	2	–	2
Paper-box making	1	1	2
Furniture making	1	–	1
Rubber	1	–	1
Electrical instruments	–	1	1
Total	8	2	10

By year, the cases involved:

– 1/1981 : a textile factory in the central region, 700 employees concerned, one arbitrator made awards on 3 issues;

– 2/1981 : a metal factory in the central region, 500 employees concerned, the parties asked to withdraw the case during appointment of arbitrators;

– 3/1981 : a metal factory in the central region, 260 employees concerned, three arbitrators made awards on 13 issues;

– 4/1981 : a textile factory in the central region, 800 employees concerned, three arbitrators made awards on 4 issues;

– 1/1982 : a furniture making factory in the central region, 288 employees concerned, one arbitrator made awards on 5 issues;

– 2/1982 : a rubber factory in the southern region, 350 employees concerned, five arbitrators made awards on 7 issues;

– 1/1984 : a paper factory in the central region, 1,222 employees concerned, three arbitrators made awards on 3 issues;

– 2/1984 : a textile factory in the central region, 1,300 employees concerned, three arbitrators made awards on 10 issues;

– 1/1985 : a paper-box factory in Bangkok, 87 employees concerned, three arbitrators made award on 6 issues;

– 1/1986 : an electrical instruments industry in Bangkok 280 employees concerned, three arbitrators made awards on 47 issues.

Note: There was no case referred to voluntary arbitration in 1983.

Other than the above cases, which were referred to voluntary arbitration under the Labour Relations Act 1975, one other dispute used voluntary arbitrators appointed according to the Civil Procedure Code.

In November 1983, an unsettled labour dispute occurred in a public enterprise. The parties to it – management and five trade unions and a employees' committee within the enterprise – agreed to appoint voluntary arbitrators. In fact, according to the Labour Relations Act this enterprise, being a public enterprise, could not use voluntary arbitrators. The conciliation officer should have referred the case to the Labour Relations Committee. But in this case the parties used the Civil Procedure Code to appoint five arbitrators; two employer's representatives, two employees' representatives and one independent member, to consider two issues. The first was the conversion of some employees' salaries from daily to monthly rates. In contention was the number of days used to calculate the month, 26 or 30. The second issue concerned the number of working-days, whether Saturday or the sixth day of the week was a holiday or not.

In June 1984, the arbitrators decided that the employer had to use 30 days or 240 hours in calculating monthly rates; the sixth day of the week was a holiday. The employer, therefore, had to pay as prescribed in the Labour Protection Law. Unfortunately, he was unable to do so because of the poor economic condition of the enterprise. Under the award, expenditures would increase by over three million dollars per month or over forty million dollars per year, even though the enterprise was losing about eighteen million dollars per year. When the employer did not follow the award, the employees struck for nine days, causing the loss of about 20 thousand mandays. Until now, however the employees have not submitted their case to the Labour Court.

ADVANTAGES OF VOLUNTARY ARBITRATION

Case Study : A labour dispute in the textile industry.

In 1981, a group representing 700 employees in a textile company in the central region, who did not organize themselves into a trade union, submitted a log of demands to the employer. The employer received the demands and the parties negotiated, but without agreement. Then the employees notified the conciliation officer but also no settlement could be reached. After that, the 700 employees went out on strike and the employer locked-out for 12 days resulting in about 8,400 mandays lost. Eventually the parties agreed to refer the case to voluntary arbitration – the first such case.

The parties appointed only one arbitrator who used only 14 days in hearing and another four days in making the award. This has been effective for not only one year as prescribed by law but even up to the present time.

From the case study above, we can point out the advantages of voluntary arbitration as follows:

As Peacemaking Machinery

According to labour dispute settlement proceedings in Thailand, the parties have the opportunity to negotiate in order to achieve a final agreement. During either negotiation or conciliation, they can try to convince or pressure each other to accept, drop or modify their demands. But whenever bargaining appears to be futile, the next step has to be considered. Voluntary arbitration, a decision-making process, is the next and final step to resolve the dispute before friction between the parties becomes serious.

As a Substitute for Work Stoppages

According to Section 34(6) of the Labour Relations Act, when a dispute which cannot be settled is pending the award of the arbitrators, neither side shall effect lock-out or strike. Thus if the parties agree to refer their case to voluntary arbitration, they renounce their rights to strike or lock-out.

As a Means to Reduce Damages Caused by Work Stoppages

As is well known, when the parties resort to work stoppages, either strike or lock-out, these actions will have an impact not only upon the parties themselves but also on the national economic situation. On the employer's side, a stoppage will cause inconvenience, loss of production, loss of profit, loss of credit and most of all, it will increase costs. On the other hand, the employees may lose their incomes. All of these effects may have an impact on national productivity (mandays lost, see table 2, loss of gross national product, willingness to improve productivity), national income, and also on social peace. Voluntary arbitration, as an alternative to work stoppages, can prevent these effects.

Table 2. Number of Labour Disputes, Strike, Lock-out and Mandays lost 1981-1985

Year	*Labour Disputes*	*Strike*	*Lock-out*	*Mandays lost*
1981	206	54	8	173,398
1982	376	22	12	116,795
1983	229	28	5	54,537
1984	86	17	10	183,698[+]
1985	220	4	6	29,857

It Follows Democratic Principles

According to the law, the parties are free to choose between work stoppages or voluntary arbitration. They are also free to select the arbitrator(s) themselves.

Justice and Acceptance

During arbitration proceedings, the tripartite arbitration board must afford both parties involved in the case the opportunity to submit argument and produce witnesses. The board must also consider all other relevant matters such as cost of living, standard of living, the consumer price index, the ability to pay of the employer, productivity changes, and prevailing practices etc. All of this should ensure that the awards will be just to both sides. So far, all parties involved in voluntary arbitration have never appealed an award nor submitted any case to Court.

It Promotes Industrial peace

Through voluntary arbitration as mentioned above, a good labour relations climate or industrial peace would be promoted.

WEAKNESSES OF VOLUNTARY ARBITRATION

As stated earlier, voluntary arbitration is still not popular. It is the most rarely used machinery of all dispute settlement methods. The reasons for its unpopularity are:

– The attitude of disputing parties towards the arbitration machinery : most of the parties prefer to resort to other means, such as political power, to pressure the other party. They are not used to a system that relies upon a third party to make a final judgement on their dispute.

Arbitrators qualifications : Experience in voluntary arbitration is still limited. The parties to a dispute are yet to be convinced of the competence, qualities, and experience of the arbitrators.

– Seldom do both parties to a dispute agree on a common arbitrator.

– Some parties to a dispute, especially the trade unions, are not satisfied with the manner of selection of arbitrators to constitute the panel. They also have no faith in the independent members appointed to the panel.

MEASURES TO INCREASE EFFECTIVENESS IN VOLUNTARY ARBITRATION.

Legal Provisions:

Some legal provisions should be reconsidered as follows:

– Parties to a dispute in vital industries should be able to refer their case to voluntary arbitration, upon the request of both parties, because during the voluntary arbitration proceedings, the parties cannot strike or lock-out;

– Time limits for hearing and making an award should be prescribed in law in order to ensure speedy voluntary arbitration proceedings.

Arbitrators:

In compiling the list of arbitrators, the following suggestions would help to ensure their acceptance by the disputing parties:

– There should be 60 names consisting of 20 employers' representatives, 20 employees' representatives and 20 independent arbitrators;

– Employers' representatives should be nominated by the Employers' Confederation. The employees' representatives should be nominated by the Labour Congress;

– The list should be re-compiled every 2 years;

– Parties to a dispute can also select arbitrators from outside the list.

In addition, arbitrators should be trained in order to enhance their knowledge and skills. They should be provided with the latest information in labour dispute settlement and should have a forum where they could exchange views and experiences.

Promotion of Voluntary Arbitration

– Include a course on voluntary arbitration in worker and management training programmes;

– Publish more information and publicise arbitration awards in order to popularise the practice. Parties to a dispute can get an idea of the quality and thinking of arbitrators from published awards, and this can facilitate selection;

– Promote its use through conciliation officers when settlement cannot be reached in conciliation.

COMPULSORY ARBITRATION

LAWS AND REGULATIONS

Besides the voluntary arbitration machinery, the first labour law, Labour Act, B.E. 2499 (1956), decreed that when a labour dispute occurs, the case shall be referred to the Labour Relations Committee for a decision or award.

The same provisions on compulsory arbitration have also appeared in every subsequent labour law, such as the Announcement of the National Excecutive Council No. 19, 1958; Proceedings for Labour Disputes Settlement Act, 1965, and Notification of the Ministry of Interior Re : Labour Relations, 1972.

At present, the legal provisions on compulsory arbitration appear in the Labour Relations Act, 1975, as follows:

– Sections 23-24 and Ministrial Regulation No. 2 B.E. 2519 (1976) which was issued under the section 23 : the kind of labour dispute that may be referred to compulsory arbitration;

– Sections 23, 30, 40, 42 and 44 : compulsory arbitration proceedings;

– Sections 37-39, 41 and 43 : Labour Relations Committee;

– Section 31-32 and 134-135 : penalty provisions.

Coverage:

According to Sections 23-24 and the Ministrial Regulation No. 2, 1976, labour disputes which cannot be settled in the following undertakings shall be referred to the Labour Relations Committee:

- Railway;
- Port;
- Telephone or telecommunication;
- Production or distribution of energy or electricity for the public;
- Production or refinery of oil fuel;
- Water Works;
- Hospital or clinic;
- All undertakings by State enterprises pursuant to the law on budgetary appropriations;
- Private colleges and schools pursuant to the law on private colleges and the law on private shools;
- Undertakings by co-operatives under the law on co-operative societies;
- Land, water and air transport as well as supplementary undertakings of transport or in connection with transport at depot, harbour and airport, and tourism,
- Sale of fuel oil pursuant to the law on fuel oil.
- Also those labour disputes which cannot be settled, or those lock-outs or strikes which the Minister of Interior considers may affect the economy of the country or cause hardship to the public or endanger the security of the country or be against public order.

Proceedings

Under the Labour Relations Act, 1975, if a labour dispute in the prescribed undertakings cannot be settled by conciliation, the conciliators shall refer the case to the Labour Relations Committee for consideration and notify both parties within thirty (30) days from the date the case is received. In the performance of its duty, the Labour Relations Committee shall have the power to appoint a Sub-committee in order to find facts and submit opinion on matters assigned to it of permanent or definite duration.

Resolutions of the Labour Relations Committee, which shall consist of not less than one-half of the total number of members and one member each from employers and employees, shall be by majority vote and each member shall have one vote. In the case of deadlock, the chairman of the meeting shall have an additional vote.

The parties to a dispute have the right to appeal a Labour Relations Committee decision to the Minister of Interior within seven (7) days. The Minister shall consider the appeal and notify both parties of his decision within ten (10) days. A decision of the Labour Relations Committee which has not been appealed within the prescribed period, and the decision of the Minister shall be final. Both parties shall comply therewith. In fact, the parties sometimes submit their case to the Labour Court.

Effective Labour Relations Committee decisions and those of the Minister shall be effective for one year. During compulsory arbitration proceedings, the parties to a dispute are not permitted to strike or lock-out.

Penalty Provisions

The penalties are the same as for voluntary arbitration.

LABOUR RELATIONS COMMITTEE

This Committee is tripartite. It consists of a Chairman and not less than eight but not more than fourteen members. Out of these numbers there must be three members from employers and three from employees.

At present (1986), the committee consists of 15 members : five each from employers and employees, three independent members, a chairman (independent member), and a secretary (independent member). Employers' and employees' members are selected from lists submitted by the national trade union congresses (Labour Congress of Thailand, National Free Labour Union Congress, The National Congress of Thai Labour, Thai Trade Union Congress) and the Employers' Confederation of Thailand. The three independent members and the chairman are chosen from retired civil servants. The secretary is a serving civil servant who also functions as Chief of the Office of the Labour Relations Committee.

Term of office

The chairman and members shall hold office for three years. At the end of the first year of the initial term, one-third of the committee shall retire by drawing lots, and the new appointees shall hold office for a term of three years. In addition, all committee members shall also vacate office upon:

- death;
- resignation;
- being dismissed by the Minister of Interior;

- being bankrupt;
- being an incompetent or quasi-incompetent person;
- being imprisoned by final judgement of imprisonment.

New appointees shall hold office for the remaining term of the chairman or members they replace.

Power and Duties

The Labour Relations Committee has the power and duties to:

- exercise the power of compulsory arbitration;
- decide labour disputes as authorized or entrusted;
- consider and decide complaints on unfair practices under section 125 of the Labour Relations Act, 1975;
- submit opinion concerning the demand, negotiation, and settlement of labour disputes, strikes and lock-outs as entrusted by Minister;
- issue meeting regulations and lay down rules of procedure for consideration and decision of labour disputes and unfair practices and for issuing the orders of the Labour Relations Committee.

In the performance of its duty, the Labour Relations Committee and its sub-committee(s) shall have the power to:

- enter the offices of an employer, place of work of employees or office of employers' association, labour union, employers' federation, or labour federation during office hours in order to inquire into facts or examine documents as deemed necessary;
- issue letters of inquiry or summon any person to give evidence or forward relevant items or documents to supplement the consideration of the Labour Relations Sub-committee.

The person concerned shall render facilities, reply to the letter of inquiry, present facts or forward relevant items or documents to members of the Labour Relations Committee or Labour Relations Sub-committee who are performing the prescribed duties.

EFFECTIVENESS OF COMPULSORY ARBITRATION

In the past, labour disputes that could not be settled and were referred to the Labour Relations Committee came to about 20 cases per year. But in the past three years the number of cases so referred has decreased to about 3-9 cases per year. During the past five years (1981-1985), a total of 60 decisions were made, 53.3 per cent of which were not appealed. In most of the remaining cases, the decisions of the Minister of Interior were complied with. Only two cases were appealed to the Labour Court. The length of time used to make a decision per case was not more than 30 days. The number of decisions, their acceptance and the average time taken during 1981 to 1985 are shown in Table 3.

Table 3. The number of decisions made by the Labour Relations Committee and acceptance of such decisions by the parties. 1981-1985

year	*1981*	*1982*	*1983*	*1984*	*1985*	*Total*
1) Number of decisions	21	19	9	3	8	60
2) Decisions which had not been appealed	13	12	2	1	4	32
3) Number of appeals to the Minister	7	6	7	2	4	26
4) Number of appeals to the Labour Court	1	1	–	–	–	2
5) Average length of period in making decision	30	30	30	30	30	30
6) Backlog of cases	–	–	–	–	–	–

IMPACT ON NEGOTIATION

According to law, compulsory arbitration is the last labour dispute settlement machinery. Before this stage, the law affords the parties the opportunity to negotiate. However, when a case cannot be settled in negotiation and in the conciliation stage in vital industries it must be referred to compulsory arbitration. So in fact compulsory arbitration has no impact upon negotiations or the collective bargaining stage. In practice, the Labour Relations Committee encourages the parties to negotiate and also conciliates the dispute, sometimes making a decision according to an agreement reached by the parties.

MEASURES TO INCREASE EFFECTIVENESS IN COMPULSORY ARBITRATION.

– At present, the law has no provisions on the qualifications of members of the Labour Relations Committee. Members names are merely submitted by employers and employees and selected by the Government. The law should add a provision on this matter.

– The length of time in making a decision should be extended as follows:

– sixty (60) days for the Labour Relations Committee;

– thirty (30) days for the Minister of Interior.

So that such decisions will be just to both parties.

– Every sub-committee appointed by the Labour Relations Committee should be a tripartite body.

– The chairman and Committee members should be trained in order to enhance their knowledge and experience in compulsory arbitration.

CONCLUSION

In comparing the two arbitration systems, their general purpose, which is the settling of labour disputes which cannot be settled by conciliation through peaceful means and as a substitute for work stoppages is similar. In practice, the board of arbitrators appointed by the parties to a dispute in the voluntary system is also a tripartite body as is the Labour Relations Committee.

The differences between the two systems are, firstly, the nature of the case according to law. The voluntary system allows freedom to disputing parties in general industries to choose between arbitration and work stoppage. But disputing parties in public utilities, essential services and those cases that may affect the economy or security of the country or public order shall not effect a lock-out nor go on strike. The dispute must be referred to compulsory arbitration. Secondly, in the voluntary system, the parties are free to select their own arbitrator(s). In the compulsory system, the case shall be considered by the Labour Relations Committee.

In comparing the acceptance of voluntary arbitrators' awards and compulsory arbitrators' decisions, although the number of decisions made by compulsory arbitrators is greater, the voluntary arbitrators' awards seem more acceptable. Their awards have never been appealed. On the other hand, half the decisions of the Committee have been appealed.

However, both systems of arbitration are equally important under law as the final labour dispute settlement machineries. Efforts should be intensified to promote both machineries, especially the popularity of voluntary arbitration.

www.ingramcontent.com/pod-product-compliance
Ingram Content Group UK Ltd.
Pitfield, Milton Keynes, MK11 3LW, UK
UKHW041850190726
13854UKWH00002B/812